DAUGHTER

of the Reformation

A HISTORICAL PERSPECTIVE OF THE LIFE
AND TIMES OF THE WIFE OF MARTIN LUTHER

DAUGHTER

of the Reformation

MARY HELENE RASMUSSEN JACKSON

DAUGHTER OF THE REFORMATION
A Historical Perspective of the Life and Times of the Wife of Martin Luther

Copyright © 2014 Mary Helene Rasmussen Jackson. All rights reserved.

Publisher: Huff Publishing Associates, LLC
Minneapolis

Book design by Hillspring Books, Inc.

The Luther ring in the illustration on the cover is a special design-reliquary produced by Annette Kienast-Kistner.

ISBN 978-0-9895277-7-4

LCCN: 2014948280

Copies of this book may be purchased through Huff Publishing Associates (www.huffpublishing.com).

Manufactured in the U.S.A.

Dedicated to my mother and my father

Jemima Helena Osheim Rasmussen

who made a warm home of ten parsonages
filled with music, ironed pillowcases, and peach jam

Pastor Henry Edmund Rasmussen Jr.

a gentle man of shining faith
who loved his Bible, his family, history, and running races

ACKNOWLEDGEMENTS

With gratitude, I thank several people who gave advice and encouragement along the way: Sharon Holmen Peterson, who started me on this journey on a single Sunday School morning many years ago; Dr. Paul Dovre and Ruth Rotto Lyngaas for their critiques and inspiration in manuscript reading; Elizabeth Jackson Kirchhoff for technical assistance; Sharon and Stephen Hoiland for German translation; and Scott Tunseth for his astute editing. I am also in debt to the many dedicated historical authors and scholars of several centuries who have searched for, discovered, and recorded countless facts about the people, named and nameless, who lived in the sixteenth century.

AUTHOR'S NOTE

History as we know it is dependent upon eyewitness accounts that may or may not be colored by personal bias and also by authentic written documents that are copied, sometimes printed, and often translated from one language to another—and maybe to another. In addition, a high percentage of recorded history comes from the male point of view, which is logical because authority—political, religious, literary, or commonplace—was usually in the hands and presented by the pens of men. As a result, the lives, influence, and thoughts of women have largely disappeared. Although the story of civilization is just as dependent upon their stories, just as much an integral part of all human experience, their lives and words from birth to death are often lost in the shadows of the centuries. How then do we write of the journey of Catharina von Bora who was born more than five hundred years ago?

To tell her story, one must often search dozens, if not hundreds, of pages about Martin Luther to come upon one fact about her. Yet, most historians agree that without her, his profound effect upon western religion and thought, resulting in the Protestant Reformation, would have been far different. While Martin Luther wrote extensively and published volumes of translations, commentaries, music, sermons, articles, and essays, she wrote neither a journal nor literary materials. Some references to letters she wrote can be found. Some written information about her from contemporaries exists. However, vast sources of documented sociological, political, biographical, and theological information about life in the sixteenth century are available. We can only hope to interweave those facts with the days of Catharina to find a portrait of who she was.

Conversational dialog before 1524 has been added within these pages so that we may meet this extraordinary woman.

Elsewhere, I ask the reader to listen between the lines. The words of German women in the 1500's were not duly written down or meant to be remembered. The words simply do not exist. Therefore, pre-Wittenberg conversation between Catharina von Bora and others in this small volume are neither annotated nor taken word for word from historical resource material. It does reflect and portray the events, customs, and known information about those days and years together with her experiences. Using facts about the years of her lifetime together with authenticated statements concerning her life from 1499 to 1552, I have tried to let Catharina live and learn again, laugh and weep again. She was not just a footnote. Names, places, and dates are taken from historical record and research and in context.

It is no small task for those studying and writing about history to breathe life into pen and paper. When John Adams was eighty years old, he wrote to Thomas Jefferson, "Who shall write the history of the American Revolution? Who will ever be able to write it?" Jefferson replied in his letter, "Nobody; except merely its external facts. The life and soul of human history must for ever be unknown." Was he right? Perhaps. But we can try.

This book is a journey to the sixteenth century to learn about the Reformation and its people whose stories are written and unwritten. The search through pages of history and beloved literature affirms the fact that faces change, but people do not.

Martin Luther's wedding ring was engraved with the initials MLD and CvB. In historical sources, his wife's name is spelled in different formal and informal ways depending upon the interpretation of the translator or research study. Variations are Katharina, Katarina, Katherina, Katerina, Katerine, Catharina, Catherine, Caterina, Këthe, Kette, and Katie. I will use the spelling "Catharina."

Mary Helene Rasmussen Jackson

"Oh, Great Spirit,
Grant that I may not criticize my neighbor until I have
walked a mile in his moccasins."

–Chief Joseph, Nez Perce Indian Tribe

TABLE OF CONTENTS

Acknowledgments   VIII
Author's Note   IX
Foreword   XIII

Prologue • 1520   1
Chapter One • April 5, 1523   19
Chapter Two • February 1503   31
Chapter Three • June 1505   35
Chapter Four • November 1508   39
Chapter Five • October 8, 1515   45
Chapter Six • 1520   59
Chapter Seven • Spring and Summer of 1517   67
Chapter Eight • 1517   85
Chapter Nine • 1483-1519   105
Chapter Ten • 1520-1523   133
Chapter Eleven • April 5, 1523   155
Chapter Twelve • 1523-1525   163
Afterward • 1526-1552   181

Postscript   221

Chronology of Catharina von Bora   224

IMAGE GALLERY

Image Credits   225
Chronology of Martin Luther   227
Literary Excerpts and End Notes   229
Bibliographic Sources   237

Foreword

This book comes to us at a propitious time, the observation of the 500th anniversary of the Reformation. And it comes to us from a remarkable author who is able to humanize the flow of history shaping people and events.

Those history shaping events will be at the center of the celebration for the life and work of Martin Luther and his colleagues who have drawn the respect and gratitude of many generations over several centuries. His influence went beyond the central premise that we are saved by grace and justified by faith. In addition, he assured believers that they had access to God without need for any intermediary and that all were called to ministry as members of a priesthood. In these years of celebration we will call attention to these central themes. And we shall also take note of Luther's contributions to church liturgy and music, his articulation of the freedom of the Christian and his emphasis on the the responsibility of citizens for the common good. We shall also revisit Luther and Melanchthon's roles as educational reformers and as advocates and exemplars of intellectual freedom and, in justice, we will recall the lessons of the late Luther with respect to the peasants and the Jews. All of this and more will provide a wonderful agenda for inquiry, celebration, and contemplation.

I submit that this volume will enrich the celebration in a unique way. Let me explain: in recent decades, post-modernists have emphasized the importance of context in shaping human behavior. With respect to Martin Luther, we have voluminous material about the ecclesial, political, and social contexts of the late Middle Ages. Likewise, we know a good deal about Luther's colleagues—his mentors, teachers, defenders, and adversaries. We know a good deal about the social hierarchy and the rude lives of the peasant class. But the significant missing links in what we know about Luther relate to the domestic context, the home and family. Yes, we know something of his father's personality, his hopes for Martin and his disappointment at his son's vocational choice. But we know considerably less about the primary relationship in his life, his wife Catharina von Bora. It is that reality which makes most welcome this volume about her life and legacy, as well as the family life of the Luthers. By attending to both what we know about the events she experienced and the circumstances in which she lived, Mary Helene Rasmussen Jackson lets Catharina live with authenticity. The result is that our understanding of Luther and the Reformation is deepened and broadened.

Jackson accomplishes this by reporting what we know about von Bora and then filling in the missing content with imagination and clarity. She does this by bringing us into the von Bora household, the Nimbschen Convent, the church of Tetzel and the Luther household. She describes the ordinary and stressful experiences of childhood, the nurture and discipline of the Convent and finally the household in which Catharina managed to create orderliness and hospitality out of chaos and confusion.

It is in the narrative of the marriage that this book excels. As the author writes: "In matters of little things and of great things, he would change her life and she would change his." This narrative lends further substance to Derek Wilson's observation that Catharina "provided him with the stability which was the launchpad for his creativity. . . . Indeed, it is difficult to see how Luther's ministry could have continued through his middle and later years without the stability and creature comforts provided by his domestic life" (*Luther: Out of the Storm*, Fortress Press 2010, 236, 238).

Jackson writes with an easy and intelligible style and in language sometimes descriptive and other times evocative. The text is enriched with excerpts from a variety of literary sources. The author brings to the project the authenticity of one who grew up in a parsonage and experienced that life first hand, most especially, the roles of the pastor and the pastor's wife, the rhythms of the parish and the flow of family life. For all of these reasons, this book will be helpful in deepening our understanding of the role of Catharina von Bora, "the Morningstar of Wittenberg," in the momentous life of her beloved Martin and the history shaping events of the Reformation.

Dr. Paul J. Dovre
President Emeritus
Concordia College

PROLOGUE

I.

Saxony in 1520. Watered by the Elbe and Saale Rivers, it was a land of rich fertile soil and deep forests within the Holy Roman Empire in northeastern Germany. The region was divided into two domains in 1485. The larger part to the north contained Wittenberg, a flourishing university town; Castle Church was its most prominent landmark. The southern portion included Leipzig and Dresden, its largest cities. They consisted mainly of small wooden structures—houses, barns, and shops. Stone was usually reserved for buildings meant to last for centuries: the churches, the monasteries, and

1

the schools of higher learning. A powerful landowner, the Roman Catholic Church, the richest in Christendom's history, owned and operated several thousand square acres, nearly a third of all landed properties, within both areas of Saxony. Personages of the upper ecclesiastical orders lived with wealth and luxury far above the great majority of the people.

Smaller villages were scattered across the countryside—Torgau, Eisleben, Grimma, Halle, Jüterbog, and Mansfeld—to name a few. Narrow graveled roads, deeply rutted with wagon wheel tracks and nearly impassable in the rainy months, were vital links of commerce and communication between the towns. Most of the population was made up of the peasants who farmed the land. Few were educated beyond making a mark to signify their names; all worked long, backbreaking hours between sunrise and sunset, coaxing the soil to produce profit for their masters, the Church or those few leisured Saxon nobility who still retained power and wealth. High taxes burdened and discouraged the poor. Simple necessities of life were unavailable or expensive; the same article of clothing was often worn for months or even years. Small timber and clay huts and cottages provided little more than a rough dirt floor, straw-plastered walls, and thatched roofs for protection from the ever-changing and often hostile weather that became bitterly cold in the winter. During the long, dark frigid nights from November until March, the whole family slept around the kitchen fire. Some farmers had their own little plots to till, but most of them were denied access to the abundant woodlands to gather firewood for cooking and heat. Nevertheless, during the summer and autumn months, theft of twigs and branches to be used for fuel was an ongoing task for the family's children. It was not unusual for the peasant property to have a chicken coop and a pigsty. A small barn sometimes provided safety for farm animals; it was common for smaller creatures to share the family hut. The forests and fish-filled streams were reserved for the masters' sport and pleasure.

Payment of taxes was a required and sometimes unbearable burden on the backs of the peasants. They paid two masters: first, a tithe or one-tenth of all grain, fruit, vegetables, and livestock to the Church each year; second, twice a year, an arranged percentage of all the peasants produced was paid to the lord for rent of the land; in addition, they gave twelve to sixty days of service whenever the lord required their labor. Even in death, the masters demanded a tax; often, the landowner grabbed half of a peasant's poor estate.

For centuries the peasants had lived according to the dictates of the sun; they rose at dawn and went to bed at sunset. During the cycle of the new moon, utter darkness covered the earth like a great black cape; the vial of night reigned in every vale and forest. The luxury of light and nighttime revelry belonged to the rich. Country weddings and town fairs did provide rare moments of celebration, but most of life was full of foreboding terrors of the dark, of demons, and of frightening superstitions. Fantasy was both dreadful and real for the people who were obsessed with the Day of Judgment and the Devil. Hunger, disease, and bad harvests clouded the minds of those who were already fearful of the unknown and of certain punishment from a wrathful God.

These people were driven to rebellion and desperation because they were no more than forgotten faces manipulated and enslaved by the ruling class, which was largely in alliance with the increasing punitive and psychological authority of the Holy Roman Church. Nevertheless, in spite of their poor position, they managed an occasional feeble but determined uprising.

The symbol of unity chosen by the peasants was a farmer's boot laced to the knee—called the Bond of the Shoe, or 𝔅𝔲𝔫𝔡𝔰𝔠𝔥𝔲𝔥. Their hero, a lowly cowherd named Hans Bohm, declared in the year 1476 that the Mother of God Herself had told him that all authorities from king to pope to cardinal to prince would disappear. All people would be free and share the bounty of the land. Although hundreds of common folk gathered and listened to his revelations, the Church paid little attention until Hans made a call for arms. Then, by order of the bishop, his soldiers arrived and arrested the madman. Threatened with superior force, the crowds scattered. This short but frustrating uprising was but a mosquito in the ear of the Church. The discontent was supposedly over. But the German serfs were not frightened into easy submission. More revolts sprang up from the Rhineland to the Polish border in 1493, 1502, 1512, and again in 1517; the peasants used axes and fire to little avail. All explosions of social unrest were systematically snuffed out and are recorded simply as fruitless bloody attempts for a better way of life. However, the arrest, torture, and hanging of many of the leaders did not quench the common man's hopes and determination. In the 1520's, the land was again ripe for an organized and far-reaching rebellion, one that would be devastating to the Church. Many had reached the point of being unafraid of bitter political conflict and the dangerous consequences of religious revival.

The common man had suffered too long in body, soul, and property. He would endure the powerful marriage of the Church and the secular landowners no longer. The enemies were as old as written Saxon history itself. But the weapons of the people were new. The weapons were these: nationalism, the printing press, and a monk named Martin Luther who rediscovered grace.

II.

The seven-hundred-year-old Holy Roman Empire, of which Saxony was a small part, stretched from the Baltic and North Seas southward across the Alps to the warm shores of the Mediterranean and adjacent to the Papal States whose crown jewel was Rome. It crowded France to the west and extended six hundred and fifty miles east into the heart of Europe. In Germany, its

Imperial crown, already worn by monarchs of the Hapsburg family sitting comfortably in Vienna for almost a century, was virtually in the hands of the territorial princes, the Electors, seven powerful men who elected or accepted the emperor. This group was made up of three archbishops of the Church and four secular princes. The emperor conducted business, made decisions to go to war, listened to complaints and requests, and asked for money and men for his intended actions. These seven Electors together with other dignitaries met with the emperor in a large city such as Nuremberg, Augsburg, or Worms.

Maximilian I, who reigned from 1493 to 1519, was emperor of the Holy Roman Empire when unrest was beginning to seriously infect the countryside. He was not a great general, was inept at finances, and was a man of mediocre intellect. He was a dreamer and hoped to be the pope as well as the emperor. On the plus side, he encouraged literature and art and possessed the unique talent of easily acquiring languages. He spoke or understood eight—German, Latin, French, Italian, Spanish, Walloon, Flemish, and English. This ability was of tremendous advantage as he married off members of his family to far-reaching royalty and thus expanded the empire greatly.

His grandson, Charles V, succeeded Maximilian in 1519. His father, Philip the Handsome and Duke of Burgundy, had married Juana of Spain. Incidentally, he turned out to be Philip the Unfaithful, and Juana gradually lost her mind in grief. He is reported to have said, "I speak Spanish to God, Italian to women, French to men, and German to my horses." Charles became Holy Roman Emperor at the age of fifteen. He sat on the throne for thirty-seven years of the Renaissance and Reformation. Remaining true to the Roman Catholic faith throughout his life, he abdicated his throne in 1556 and withdrew to pray and die in a monastery in Spain.

Meanwhile, the comforts enjoyed by the titled did not enter the walls of the farmer's hut and hamlet. Not surprisingly, the peasants were a sullen lot who continued to take every opportunity to get out from under the heavy physical and psychological yoke of feudalism and the control of those contemporary rulers who were disinterested in their lives. A new national character was developing, and it did not include loyalty to a faraway court nor to a distant papacy.

The secular and ecclesiastical princes, sinking in moral decay, ruled in confusion, grasping all the money and riches they could collect and keep in their own coffers, thereby sending as little gold as possible to Vienna and Rome. Furthermore, an emerging manufacturing and mercantile class was giving rise to organizations of solidarity as well as protection for businesses and the demand for private ownership; let the Holy Roman Church find its own money-making opportunities! Augsburg became the financial center where several banking dynasties were developing and thriving. The emperor's knights were but a shadow of their former honorable selves. Instead of being known for virtue and bravery, their reputation became one of inept and cruel power ploys. In fact, many of them were highwaymen and preyed upon citizens who traveled the unprotected roads between villages.

The medieval order was collapsing. And the Church, holding hands under and over the table with the Hapsburg court, was no better off. It dealt with heretics by burning them; yet, it could not break them even as the flames and suffocating smoke rose in the sky and covered the sun. And the popes of the moment played scene-stealing roles determining the future of common man without placing a satin-slippered foot within a Saxon hut nor on a stony village pathway.

Western civilization does owe much of its survival during the Dark Ages to the Roman Catholic Church. During the last half of the first millennium when Europe was foundering in ignorance, instability, and lethargy, the Church fostered community, charity, architecture, music, and preservation of education. The monastics, hidden behind their walls from the continent's chaos and deterioration, laboriously copied and protected the ancient Greek and Roman classics, and they preserved fine art for the ages. Only a few hundred years from the origin of its faith, the monasteries were the bulwark for morality, faith, learning, and order. English historian, Thomas Babington Macauley, wrote in 1873:

> There was, then, through the greater part of Europe, very little knowledge, and that little was confined to the clergy. Not one man in five hundred could have spelled his way through a psalm. Books were few and costly. The art of printing was unknown. Copies of the Bible, inferior in beauty and clearness to those which every cottager may now command, sold for prices which many priests could not afford to give. It was obviously impossible that the laity should search the Scriptures for themselves ... but a change took place. Knowledge gradually spread among the laymen.

Then a succession of both weak and strong popes, both pompous and pious, both militaristic and scholarly, both amorous and celibate, began to raise the impressive grandeur of the Holy See and oversee internal decay. As continuing decades and centuries passed, the Vatican had amassed much wealth, property, and political control. Gradually, the religious leadership was vandalized by pride and greed. Throughout recorded history, it has been a rarity that human beings can be invested with power and position and remain true to the honorable philosophy or religion that brought them there. In this case, the result was a far cry from the simple directive of Jesus, "Love one another." In 1311, William Durand, Bishop of the Council of Vienne wrote, "The whole Church might be reformed if the Church of Rome would begin by removing evil examples from herself ... the clergy feast more luxuriously ... than princes and kings." But the occupant of the papal chair continued to have authority second only to God. Higher than the angels, he must be obeyed.

Even as Rome gathered its gold from the territories of its far-reaching control, peasant and patrician unrest was no longer just an idea; it was a fact. The Protestant Reformation did not begin in 1517 with the posting of the 95 Theses. Sincere reforms requiring tremendous courage had been attempted two hundred years earlier within the Church and had failed. Secular humanist philosophers called for wide-reaching change and suggested that the Church had no business owning property, which they felt should be administered by the emperor. Further, they suggested that Scripture should be interpreted by elected Councils, not by those who purchased their Vatican positions. In the middle 1300s, Edward III of England told Pope Clement VI "that the successor of the Apostles was commissioned to lead the Lord's sheep to pasture, not to fleece them." And the riches piled up.

Erasmus of Rotterdam, a forerunner of Luther who agreed and disagreed with him as a fellow Augustinian monastic, was passionate about libraries, classical literature, and philosophic studies. This brilliant scholar startled the clerics with his praise of Epicurus. As a prolific lecturer and writer, he translated the Greek New Testament into Latin, and he dared to show his true colors about certain impious Church fathers in his satirical book, "The Praise of Folly," which was devoured by university students throughout Europe in a dozen translations. Amongst his opinions and writings: "There are shocking contrasts between the Christianity of the Church and the Christianity of Christ ... Would that men were content to let Christ rule by the laws of the Gospel, and that they would no longer seek to strengthen their obscurant tyranny by human decrees! ... In this part of the world I am afraid a great revolution is impending."

In the 1400s, widespread citizen dissatisfaction and disillusionment permeated the land. St. Barnardino wrote, "Very many folk ... believe in nothing higher than the roofs of their houses." The Council of Pisa in 1411 did try to restore the papacy to honor by demanding the removal of Pope John XIII as a "pagan, oppressor, liar, traitor, lecher, thief," and sixteen more sins. Year by year, denunciations of Rome became louder. The accomplished and sincere Cardinal Nicolas of Cusa called for serious reform with like-minded theologians and tried to cut through the gloom, but there was little consequence. The chasm between the supremacy of the pope and the despair of the peasant was becoming an abyss. In 1513 in his *Discourses* iii.I, Machiavelli added his words to the chorus:

> Had the religion of Christ been preserved according to the ordinances of the Founder, the state and commonwealth of Christendom would have been far more happy than they are ... And whoever examines the principles on which that religion is founded and sees how widely different from those principles its present practice and application are, will judge that her ruin or chastisement is near at hand.

Rome saw four popes between the years of 1510 and 1534. Julius II of Liguria, whose grandfather was a poor fisherman, lived a far different lifestyle from his ancestor and was determined to resurrect the glory of Rome. He was a tall commanding man with a quick temper, known to carry a stick with him to beat anyone who displeased him. As a cardinal, he had enjoyed several mistresses and become the father of three daughters. As pope, his determined dream was to build a new St. Peter's Basilica atop the ruins of the old crumbling church that had been commissioned by Constantine centuries before. In 1506, he hired a brilliant architect, Donato Bramante, to design the building, laid the cornerstone for the new church, and proceeded to raise the funds to build it. By 1513, 70,000 gold ducats to be spent on construction were obtained from loans from wealthy bankers, gifts from crowned heads of Europe, and indulgences—the St. Peter's Indulgence in particular. Henry VIII of England, then a solid son of Rome, donated the tin for the roof and received wine and Parmesan cheese in return. Pope Julius II also passionately supported the arts and commissioned Michelangelo to paint the ceiling of the Sistine Chapel as well as to construct a lavish three-story papal tomb for himself that would display forty statues and be built of 100 tons of marble. The money for the project ran out, the basilica and the tomb were unfinished, and the Pope died in 1513. He was to be surpassed in pomp.

The new pope, Giovanni de Medici, known as Pope Leo X, played a central role in the story of the Reformation. At the age of sixteen, this son and heir of the powerful House of Medici had been made a cardinal. As a child, he had studied and played games in the family courtyard with the young Michelangelo who lived under the roof of the Medicis. Leo's father, Lorenzo, had recognized the developing artist's genius and became Michelangelo's patron. On the day that Leo became pope, he entered the Vatican in an extravagant parade. The streets and houses were decorated with scarlet velvet banners and laurel wreaths, and he was hailed as the "Ambassador of Heaven." Riding on a white Arabian stallion past fountains that were spraying wine rather than water, he was preceded by soldiers in full regalia, prelates bearing jeweled crowns, white mules, and bishops and cardinals on white draped horses. The day was only a prelude to unencumbered spending. Within a year, still a Medici, he had spent almost all that was in Rome's strongbox. It had gone for gambling, hunting, lavish gifts of gold to friends, and great banquets. To his credit, Leo also restored ancient churches and encouraged scholarship and the use of his family library. Aware of the sure celebrity of Michelangelo, he tried to reconnect with his old playmate, but the artist would have none of it. Leo retorted, "He is an alarming man. There is no getting on with him." Largely due to his burning ambition to complete St. Peter's, Pope Leo faced theological, political, and historical problems of monumental magnitude in his far-reaching territories.

At his death in 1521, Leo X was followed by Pope Hadrian VI, a man of even temper and prayer who lived only until 1523, and later by Pope Clement VIII, a patron of the arts and politician of purpose who finally cleaned up the streets of Rome and was witness to the bonfire of events that heralded the Reformation.

To the north of Germany, Scandinavia was becoming a bastion for Protestantism and was also slowly but surely preparing national ground for the approaching reformation of the Church. The papacy owned half of Denmark; it was no revelation that the increasing wealth of the church which was exempt from taxation caused anticlerical sentiment to grow. In addition, serfdom was on its way out in Norway and Sweden, despite poorly organized peasant rebellions. Norway had experienced a unique opportunity for stability in government amidst all the chaos in Europe when the prudent and remarkable Regent Margaret governed for more than thirty years until the year 1412. Her wavering successors then presided over Norway's decline with weak leadership, and it would sleep under the tightening political control of Denmark even as Rome lost its influence in those far northern lands.

The revolt against unscrupulous control and dogma beyond reason was about to shake the western world to its very core. Religious sterility and subservience to figureheads were no match for the new spirit of hope for a better life. Nationalism, rather than local patriotism and papal obeisance, was being born. But it would not have succeeded in its birth pangs without the grand invention, the printing press.

III.

Printing with movable wooden type was an ancient art, used in China and Korea as early as the eleventh century. However, it was of little value for those Asian vernaculars that consisted of several thousand characters. Such was not the case for the languages of Europe, which used the Roman alphabet. By the 1400's, presses with movable metal type were being set up in Holland

and in Germany. Developed by Johann Gutenberg, a citizen of Strasbourg and Mainz, and his employees, the wonderful new invention was at first welcomed with great enthusiasm. In 1456-7, Gutenberg printed over forty copies of his majestic 1282-page volume of the Bible in a monumental effort that was to herald the birth of learning and communication for the common people.

When the art of printing spread quickly throughout Germany and further on to printing shops from Rome to England to Sweden, rulers and the clergy panicked and feared that it would disperse and multiply rebellious ideas counter to their own purposes and tenets. Copyists were certain that making inexpensive books available to just anybody would destroy their trade. And the rich who owned manuscript libraries were convinced that their print possessions would be considered common.

The press was here to stay. It became a priceless vehicle for the peasants in their fight to throw off the heavy burden of serfdom because it was the first time in history that education was even remotely possible for the general populace. Pamphlets, personal letters, broadsheets, and songs with cryptic verses were published by the thousands and purchased by anyone with a penny in his pocket. The printed word became the glue that held thousands of "nobodies" together in their noble quest for dignity. Further, the printing press marked the end of the Church's iron-fisted control of learning. Up to and throughout the thirteenth century, only the monastics could read. At that time, universities throughout Europe were established, primarily for males, and taught in large part by the clergy. In contrast, by 1500, literacy was emerging in the middle and upper classes; even some noble-women were setting aside their needlework and prided themselves in owning silk and leather-bound books which they were learning to read, usually under the tutelage of nuns from the convents.

The peasants' freedom to read was a dreaded chalice of poison for the Holy Roman Empire; it was an exhilarating instrument of change for the people. And in 1521-22, while hiding from the papacy in the ancient and massive Wartburg Castle and using the alias of Junker Jörg, a monk from Eisleben named Martin Luther translated the New Testament into the earthy Saxon tongue of the masses. Because of the timely invention of the printing press, one hundred thousand copies of the translation were distributed throughout the land. The Bible became the possession of the people! To the horror of the Mother Church, they dared to listen to or read it without the guidance and sanctioned interpretation of priests.

IV.

The priest to be reckoned with was an Augustinian monk, Martin Luther, who chose to challenge the might and a good deal of the accepted history of the Church. In the printed and distributed Edict of Worms, according to the twenty-year-old Emperor Charles V, heir to the Holy Roman Empire, Luther's heretical indiscretion was that "He makes the sacraments depend upon the faith of the recipient. He denies the power of the keys. He recognizes only the authority of Scripture, which he interprets in his own sense." Judgment followed. "No one is to harbor him. His followers also are to be condemned. His books are to be eradicated from the memory of man!"

Rarely has a royal proclamation been so soundly ignored. This monk from Wittenberg, the pride and joy and hope of his strict and superstitious father until he tossed away a legal future for an academic and monastic life, could not be silenced. His religious and intellectual curiosity together with his depth of conscience would not permit it. The man was frustrated and driven to despair by the direction of the paternalistic Church. Was it still a true representative of the Jesus that he loved so dearly? It was his own uncertainty that prompted him to challenge the very foundation of the Church, hoping that reason, sound scholarship, and simple faith would reverse the certain materialistic destruction of Christendom. It was not his purpose to lead a rebellion, but to facilitate a religious revival and reformation from within. Even so, the times were ripe for revolt. Peasant insecurity was bolstered by a good deal of successful insolence and violence and, finally, the confidence to spark the explosion of social unrest that went far beyond theological debate. Change of monumental proportions was in the wind, and neither Martin Luther nor the young Hapsburg emperor nor the Pope in Rome nor any German Elector nor even more than a thousand years of entrenched Roman Catholic tradition could do anything to stop it.

The fire was lit some years before Martin Luther posted his 95 Theses in 1517. Unwittingly, a loud and pseudo-pious Dominican monk by the name of Johann Tetzel swung the doors of the Church wide open so that Luther could stride through. Tetzel was the original slippery Christian salesman. He sold salvation. In the names of the Father, Son, and Holy Ghost and, incidentally, the Holy See, he traded beautifully printed documents of redemption for money. These papers, called indulgences, restored innocence and purity to those who were already dead, to those who erred in secret last night, and even to the penitent soul who planned to sin tomorrow. As he swept into the villages of Germany, elders, magistrates, and priests with tinkling bells and waving banners joined him as they marched through the streets to gather the townspeople. Even the convents and monasteries were emptied of their nuns and monks who were permitted to join the parade of sinners soon to be sanctified if they had enough silver in their purses.

Tetzel's mistake was to wander boldly into the territory of Saxony. When buyers of his paper forgiveness asked the respected professor and lecturer at the University of Wittenberg, Dr. Martin Luther, for theological approval of the whole business, he roared a resounding "No!" He had had enough. No more could or would he abide the flagrant abuses of the Holy Roman Church. And so, according to academic custom, he declared his opposition by writing in Latin and then posting his 95 Theses on the splendid door of Castle Church. He formally requested rebuttal from anyone interested in debating the subject and allowed distribution of copies in the German language to the populace because, in his opinion, they were the ones who had been hoodwinked by Tetzel. The date was October 31, 1517. The protests of those who believed that all men and women could be their own priests were about to be heard.

Year after year after year, the poor of Europe had been trod underfoot. Though they bled when hurt, trembled when frightened, ached when hungry, and laughed when full of mirth—just like the lace-collared nobility—these men, women, and children simply disappeared like smoke, and they did not matter.

In the early sixteenth century, these simple peasants finally saw a viable champion for their very bodies and souls. Justification by personal faith, neither by deeds nor clinking coins, gave credence and returned dignity to the common man after centuries of being misused and lost in the depths of power, politics, and the papacy. The Western world would never be the same again.

V.

And so, in the year 1520, rural Saxony was the unlikely scene for the march of independent thought and faith. To further set the stage, related events that would one day be called historical milestones had already occurred or were now happening. Jeanne d'Arc had been dead for ninety years, burned at the stake for refusing to bow to the commands of Rome. Four hundred more years would pass before the Church that had killed her would canonize her. Just thirty years previous, Christopher Columbus, filled with adventure of the unknown and a lust for power, had trod upon the sands of the New World. Thinking it was the

Orient, he delivered the destiny of its native peoples to the Spanish Catholic monarchs, Ferdinand and Isabella. Balboa had laid covetous and incredulous eyes on the glorious blue span of the Pacific Ocean. Ponce de Leon had searched the North American mainland for the elusive Fountain of Youth only seven years before in 1513. By 1519, Charles V and his royal Spanish relatives dominated the European world with unequalled financial power grounded in the undreamed-of quantities of silver and gold harvested from the mines and monuments of Montezuma and the Incas. The greed for gold and desire for property in the New World claimed in the name of one crowned head or another in Europe was just beginning.

Knowledge and flowering of the arts, emerging relentlessly towards the height of the Renaissance, burst upon the continent of Europe in 1520. Musical instruments were still simple and personal. Most of the music in countryside and church was provided by the human singing voice, the recorder, drums, and the medieval fiddle. The pipe organ was in its infancy, and its keys were as broad as a man's hand. The great-grandmother of the piano, the clavichord, would not be built for twenty more years. The clarinet, violin, and brass instruments with valves had not yet been invented. In Italy, the extraordinary intelligence of sixty-seven-year-old Leonardo da Vinci had been stilled only the year before, but the world was already aware of his singular contributions to the beauties of science and art. The sculptor and painter of glorious accomplishment and genius, Michelangelo, had completed his powerful masterpiece, The Last Judgment, soaring high on the ceiling of the Sistine Chapel in the Vatican in 1512, and he was now forty-five years old.

Meanwhile, Henry VIII, England's merry monarch, wed to the first of his six wives, Katherine, Princess of the Kingdoms of Castile and Aragon and Queen of England, was thirteen years away from banishing the Pope and his defenders from the Roman cathedrals of Britain so that he could marry his Anne Boleyn in good Protestant conscience. Now, in 1520, he stormed against Martin Luther's challenge of the papacy. The English king loudly declared that no punishment could be too great for one who would not obey the Chief Priest and Supreme Judge on earth, Christ's only vicar, the Pope of Rome. Elizabeth I, his powerful daughter who would one day wear the crown of the Tudors and be declared the uncontested head of the Protestant Church of England, would not make her entrance into the world for another thirteen and a half years. Out in King Henry's countryside, William Shakespeare's father was also unborn; the Bard's grandfather, Richard Shakespeare, a hard-working tenant farmer who could not write his own name, rented land near the small English village of Snitterfield.

VI.

This is the story of Europe and its peoples as they struggled to throw off the ancient darkness of superstition, ignorance, and a powerful Church in the second and third decades of the sixteenth century. And in April of 1523, a young nun in Saxony lit her own candle.

Curtain up.

CHAPTER·ONE

Katerina von Bora dwelt in this convent from 1509 to 1523. She was liberated on 4 April 1523 by Councillor Leonhard Koppe of Torgau, and married Dr. Martin Luther in Wittenberg on 13 June 1525.

–tablet on the ruins of Nimbschen Convent

APRIL 5, 1523

I.

Near the midnight hour before Easter Sunday, the night of the full moon, shadows had already enveloped the old stone buildings of the Cistercian Cloister of Marienthon (Mary's Throne), also known as Nimbschen Convent near Grimma, Germany. Stillness settled into the clay cracks of the walls and the bell tower of the Abbey. The busy murmuring of the nuns in the kitchen and the gardens was over for another day, and the birds had long ceased their chirping in the budding pear and apple trees of the orchards. Five hours had passed since the evening prayers, and the *In Nomine* had been sung by the entire company of sisters.

In the simply furnished cells, candles were extinguished. But the full moon's bright and luminous beams softly found their way into the farthest corners of each small room so that most of the women slept, and some snored, with loosely woven blankets covering their heads.

II.

In the first years of Christian history, it was common for devout women to freely give their hearts, hours, property, and lives to those in need. These women were single, deserted, or widows; some took their vows as a refuge of silence and solitude. As the centuries passed, Benedictine convents became homes and havens for many women. With prayer and love, with humility and determination, they served as the angels of the poor. The Cistercian Orders, numbering almost 700 in Europe, were mainly composed of women from the noble or upper classes. Many of them understood poverty because their own families had become destitute. One of these convents was the wealthy Cistercian Convent of Marienthron at Nimbschen.

Nimbschen Convent had stood on a hillside in the beautiful rolling valley for more than two hundred and fifty years—since 1258. Deep woods, sparkling rushing streams, and quiet meadows surrounded it. Outside its tall thick stone walls were orchards, a large vegetable acreage, flower gardens, fishponds, and pastures of livestock, including a flock of nearly seven hundred sheep, thirty horses, and many pigs. Within the convent's confines were a mill, chicken coops, a slaughterhouse, a smithy, and a bakery. As many as forty servants toiled there along-side the nuns. Unlike the holy sisters, however, each night they returned to their own cottages and families, to their own private beds, and to their legends and habits, their own lives.

Within the property, but separated from the rest of the build-ings and land, was the close, a square area that contained the old church known as the Abbey, the sisters' dormitory, the refectory where meals were served, and the House of the Abbess, Mother Margarethe von Haubitz, who was considered by all to be a stern, pious, and honest woman. She governed the nuns accord-ing to the strict discipline of the religious order which honored the memory and virtues of St. Bernard of Clairveaux. By her discretion, she could bestow rare approval, or, when punishment was in order, compel a wayward sister to fast, to spend long days in solitary and penitential confinement, to be whipped, to observe silence for long periods of time, or to be expelled from the convent.

The forty-odd nuns and novices between the ages of nine and over eighty years old, all of noble blood, visited with mem-bers of their immediate families only twice each year by com-munication permitted through small barred windows. No small gifts of remembrance or material value could be passed through the ever-present bars, since the vice of property was surely a snare of the devil. The lowly handmaidens of the Church vowed to find no joy in possessions; the pains of poverty honorably and properly replaced the trials of the outside world, from suffering the pangs of giving birth to the struggle and weariness of sim-ple survival. Pleasure was found in separating oneself from the dangers of earthly vanities.

Originally, the order was completely dependent upon the charitable contributions of others; begging for bread in the streets by the sisters was common. Indeed, it was the only source of sustenance and survival. As years and decades and lifetimes passed, the order gradually changed to a self-sustaining part of the community. Townspeople were employed; farming and industry existed for profit; success in these ventures added money to the treasury of Rome. The women within lived in an Eden of poverty.

Life in the convent was solidly grounded in order, obedience, and the sure knowledge that tomorrow would be just like today; today was a quiet copy of yesterday. A girl who took her vows as a teenager had the expectation, and with good reason, of knowing exactly how her "Hours" would be spent, what she would wear, and how many times a day she would pray until she became forty years old, fifty years old, or by the generous grace of God, seventy. There would be no surprises for the dedicated handmaiden of the faith, nor would there be the slightest uncertainty as to what her future would be. Throughout her years from adolescence to old age, her simple needs of clothing and sustenance and pastoral care would be met. What more could one need?

There was a price to be paid. The final vows taken by the dedicated sisters were irreversible on pain of excommunication, being flung from the Holy Mother Church into a perpetual night of shame, fear, and eternal separation from God.

The lives of the nuns of Grimma, from the moment of accepting marriage to the Heavenly Bridegroom, consisted of poverty, humility, chastity, and service sprinkled with the study of elementary writing, some reading, a bit of Latin, a good deal of sewing, and singing. Throughout the day, tasks were interrupted for the chanting of sacred melodies and words from the Matins to the Lord's Prayer to the Completorium. Those who were adept at detail used their skill to illuminate religious manuscripts and embroider beautiful tapestries and delicate altar coverings. Monks depended upon the women to sew and provide them with the clothing they wore. A few of the older nuns, trained as caretakers and nurses of the sick and dying within the convent and out in the countryside, passed their potions and poultices and prayers on to carefully chosen younger women who exhibited selfless love for the newborn and dying, the diseased and crippled.

Special occasions did permit some social interaction with the monks in the nearby Augustinian monastery. In fact, many of the boys and men were brothers, uncles, or cousins of the women at Nimbschen. All the members of the holy orders were quite aware that their lives would be bleak, but, hopefully, blessed with self-sacrifice.

Such was the life of the brides of the Church; from all outward indications, they were contented souls who had found total fulfillment and purpose in their journey to heaven. It was quite beyond belief that disillusionment or unrest from the occasional peasant uprisings could ever pierce the sturdy convent walls. Centuries of barely changing traditions would surely continue day after day, year by year.

The Abbey was of special cultural and high religious significance to the community. Finely embroidered paraments, intricately and lovingly sewed by the nuns, covered its twelve altars. Of utmost importance were the treasures contained within the altars—367 precious relics in all from the vast family of saints and from the most holy places of Christendom, more than any other church in that part of Germany. Earth from the Mount of Olives and from the tomb of Joseph of Arimathea was hidden in silver-plated caskets. The robe of the honored St. Elizabeth of Thuringia, the woman whose name was synonymous with charity, lay in a finely carved chest. There were tiny priceless pieces of the Bethlehem stable, of the crown of thorns, and even from the cross of the crucifixion! The townspeople also knew that the altars protected shreds of the dress of the sinful woman, a vial of blood of the apostle Paul, and slivers of teeth and bones of many blessed saints. Perhaps the most treasured objects were pieces of the Virgin Mary's veil, too sacred to view except on extraordinary church festival days. When ancient holy hymns were chanted before the relics, when sincere and lengthy prayers were offered in that remarkably blessed Abbey, an indulgence of pardon from forty days in purgatory for a heavy sin, or a whole year for a small error, was granted. Priest and peasant alike, sinners all, traveled to the hallowed altars to be released from the weighty burdens of their failures and omissions.

After the sun set each evening, the women sang the Vesper and Completorium. Before retiring, those honored as watchers of the relics made certain that all was safe; their responsibility was immense, but gladly accepted. Night after night as darkness spread over the German countryside, after the last soft scurrying footfalls of the nuns echoing from altar to altar had disappeared, a great and noble silence stood guard over the treasures of Nimbschen. Another day was gone and tomorrow, thankfully, there would be all of the same things to do again.

III.

That Saturday night in early April of 1523, the ancient church was still, but not dark. Light from the full cold moon painted long blue watercolor shadows that silently moved across the alcove where the altars stood along the walls of the nave. Tiny orange flickering pinpoints of light from the eternal chalices further illuminated the delicate needlework that lay upon and under the holy objects.

Not far away, in one of the cells of the dormitory, a single candle still burned. Sculpted by sudden gusts of the wind into ever-changing shapes, the wax dripped and spattered down the taper and onto the brass holder. The room itself was situated near the rear of the living quarters on the ground floor. Only a few yards away, outside the small window of the sleeping chamber, rose the tall ivy-covered wall that protected the entire perimeter of the convent. Beyond it, a dusty dirty road led to the forested Saxon properties surrounding the village of Grimma.

Furnished with a low wooden cot, a plain oak chest with three drawers, and a sturdy straight chair, the small room had roughly plastered walls that were bare except for a wooden crucifix and a peg upon which hung a black woolen cloak. The candle flame cast scattered dancing patterns into the corners of the room as the chilly spring breeze played with it and gently rattled the hinges of the single open window.

A twenty-four year old nun knelt on the cold stone floor before the cross. She was dressed in the Cistercian garb of her order—a white cassock and robe tied with a black cord, a black veil covering her shorn hair and reaching halfway down her back, gray woolen socks, and heavy brown shoes. She prayed softly, then quickly rose, put on the cloak, and went to her window. She leaned far out over the casement and listened. Only the wind, no other sign, passed through a great pine tree near the wall. Only the wind.

IV.

The grasping hand of winter did not want to let go that year. The month of March had broken promise after promise of the coming of spring. The gray dirty snow melted down to ice, only to be covered again by another blast of stinging sleet. Impatient children cried, "Will the warm sun never come?" The farmers, however, with lifetimes of wisdom, trust, and experience were content to let nature tease them; they knew that the days would lengthen, and the soil would soften and be ready for the seeding. These folks with calloused cracked hands were capable of enduring crisis or disappointment of weather and circumstance in stolid and accepting silence. Life was short and not easy. If a German woman reached the age of forty years, it was cause for celebration; difficult childbirth and disease, war and ignorance took their toll. Tears were shed, of course, for sadness' sake, but the true finger of rage was quietly pointed at unjust manipulation and judgment by the powerful authorities of state, masters, and Church. Such thoughts were usually planted and protected deep within. Such pain did not often spill over into rebellion. The people usually conformed without much question. This was their way.

Constant fear of the devil and frustration with poverty were the emotions that the peasants allowed to surface. Young and old alike, before traveling on an unknown road or when passing over the threshold of their cottage door, repeated, "Satan, I defy thee." Then, no Evil could hurt them. Terrifying superstitions and centuries-old beliefs governed their daily lives:

"It is no small remedy to cure melancholy; rub your body all over with nettles."

"If someone is bit by a mad dog, take the liver of the dog and let the patient eat it and it will help."

"If blood runs out of the body, it will be perfectly stopped if hog's dung yet hot is wrapped up in fine cotton linen, and put into the nostrils."

"If you take the bones of a female weasel and hang them over the head of a woman, she will be barren; remove them and she will be with child."

"If you would have a woman or maid to tell you all that ever she did, take the heart of a pigeon, the head of a frog, and dry and powder them; throw the powder upon the breast of her that is asleep, and she will tell all."

"To find a thief, bake the powder of an eagle bone in brown bread and give it to one which you suspect; the thief can never swallow the bread."

"Some think the woman will not miscarry if a worm that is found in the grass, before it touch the bare ground, be hanged about her neck."

"They report that when the belly is pained, if you apply a
living duck to your belly, the disease will pass into the duck,
and she will die, but you shall be cured."

"The young brother of the King of France had a most filthy
ulcer and extreme foul; he was cured by the continual
breath on it of a boy of twelve years old."

It was a well-accepted fact that there were fearsome witches who
sat by the fireside and, on moonlit nights, would often fly and
wander far and wide to dance. At worst, they cast all manner
of horrible spells and treachery upon the common man, made
women barren, caused havoc among the farm animals, and
sent plagues upon the crops. But the peasants were not afraid
of the games played by the seasons; the cycles of nature could
be trusted. Satan and all his hordes of evil angels had no power
there.

V.

It was the cold fresh smell of the dirt and last autumn's wet leaves
that placed a gentle smile on the face of the young woman. It
smelled good! Fresh and clean and honest! It brought with it
long-hidden but distinct and delightful little-girl memories of her
mother's strong hands showing her how deep to plant flower
seeds in the warm black earth and, for some reason, her father's
happy voice calling her name: "Catharina!" Oh, yes, the thaws
of spring would come and bring with them purpose and hope!
Spring would come and summer after. Closing her eyes, the nun
breathed deeply, then listened intently again. She did not hear
the sound that she sought.

Catharina turned from the window to kneel once more
before the cross. With an uplifted face, her clear blue eyes and

strong youthful countenance clung to the crucifix as she spoke aloud the words from her beloved Psalm 31:

In Thee, oh Lord, do I put my trust;
    Never let me be ashamed.
Deliver me in Thy righteousness.
Be Thou my strong rock for Thou art my fortress;
Therefore, for thy Name's sake
    Lead and guide me.

Her hands dropped to her sides, and in a trembling and desperate voice she continued to speak. "My Heavenly Father, I have tried. I have tried to be the holy sister that I promised to be. But, in all good conscience, I cannot stay here any longer. My heart is weeping because my soul is dying. I am convinced that you understand. Hear my humble words, dear Lord."

In great distress, Catharina stood up, kissed the pierced feet of the Christ on the crucifix, and ran again to the window. She clenched her hands so tightly together that the knuckles were white; she bit her lip until it hurt and then continued to whisper in prayer, "Be with us tonight as we leave this place. We go with only the clothes on our backs and our hearts and our minds. I am afraid. I don't know what lies beyond the wall anymore; I do know that I must go. Father in heaven, protect us from all our dreadful enemies and the mighty powers of the devil, if it is Thy will. Deliver us to safety, so that we might fully accept your love and grace."

Swallowing a sob, the young woman took a deep healing breath and collected herself. Finally, feeling confident of her decision and determined to retain the inner strength she knew would be severely tested in the coming hours, she freed her inborn sense of adventure and independence, so often discouraged and prohibited. With a soft but firm voice, she ended the prayer to her God. "Oh, Father, I pray that some way, somehow, you will find a place for me out there. In Thy Holy Name, Amen." At peace, she sincerely meant every word she uttered.

VI.

Her given name was Catharina von Bora, daughter of Hans der Jungere von Bora and Catharina von Haubitz, born on January 29, 1499. With knights of the western provinces of Germany for ancestors, her family was, by inheritance, part of the Saxon nobility and had been granted a coat of arms. Their farm, known as Zulsdorf near Lippendorf, could be found about six miles south of Leipzig. Their fortune, however, was like that of most titled family lines—of no consequence. Catharina's mother had died when the little girl was only four years old.

CHAPTER TWO

Into thy hands, Lord, I commend my spirit. O Lord, Jesus Christ, receive my spirit. Holy Mary, pray for me. Mary, Mother of grace, Mother of mercy, do thou protect me from the enemy and receive me at the hour of my death.

—final administration of the Eucharist

FEBRUARY 1503

I.

The bitter winter night was freezing cold and blustery. Six miles south of Leipzig and located at the edge of the town of Lippendorf stood a rambling farmhouse that had once been of some prominence and substance.

Three small children, Clemens, Little Hans, and Catharina, huddled together on the huge smooth stone hearth of the great kitchen fireplace. A big feather quilt was wrapped around their shoulders to provide some warmth. The large logs in the fireplace had been reduced to glowing embers; the fire had not been tended to for some hours.

The door opened from the next room, and their father, Hans von Bora, slowly entered with heavy steps and approached the children. They could hear sounds of subdued sobs from the dimly lit adjoining room. The father sighed from the depths of his being as he knelt and gathered the three into his arms. The children looked up and said nothing. They dared not make any sound that might intrude upon his grief. Catharina raised her small arms and touched the tears of her strong father. Little Hans grabbed one large hand with his two small ones.

"My sons and dear little Catharina," the man said in his deep gentle voice, "Your mother is dead."

And the father permitted his children to comfort him in his sorrow.

After a few moments, Father von Bora took the children by their hands into the next room. Three women and a priest were in the deathbed chamber, lit only by the light of four candles. Two of the women were aunts of the children. They were also members of a holy order. Margarethe von Haubitz, a tall dark-eyed woman, wore the Cistercian robes of an Abbess. She was the sister of the dead woman. The other nun, Magdalena von Bora, her round face better made for laughing than for crying, was sister to Hans von Bora. She was garbed in the veil and robe of a Cistercian nurse. Both women softly wept and whispered prayers as they fingered their rosary beads.

The third woman, a wrinkled aged peasant and servant of the household who usually ordered the children about from early morning to nightfall, knelt and leaned against the old trunk at the foot of the bed. She said no words, but her deeply lined face spoke of the years of memories, the decades of caring, of a lifetime dedicated to the warmth and wellbeing of her mistress. The village priest stood near the bed. His soft steady voice chanted the solemn words of the *Nunc Dimittis* and *viaticum*. He had already placed a coin in the dead mother's mouth as provision for the journey to convey her soul across the river that separated the living from the dead. He whispered her final prayer for her in her ear, "Receive me in the hour of my death."

Hanging on the bedpost nearest the window, a stick with three impaled sun-dried frogs caught Catharina's eye. She shuddered at the sight of this remedy suggested by the apothecary to prevent further disease from entering the sickroom. It was also meant to draw all poison from the afflicted woman so that the malady would disappear.

Herr von Bora led his children to the bed. He lifted Catharina up to see the body of her mother.

"Kiss her forehead, little one," he said softly.

The girl looked at the unmoving ashen face. The thick braids were undone. Every morning, Catharina had watched her mother toss her hip-long hair over her head to comb it with long firm strokes, braid it into shiny silken plaits, and secure it in coils behind her ears. Now, the long brown hair lay tousled around her mother's head like a wreath. Then the little child gasped, cried out, and covered her eyes, for around the neck of her mother was a thin cord and tied onto it were the feet of a great toad. These had been cut off while the toad had been alive on the night of no moon and placed there by the apothecary. It was believed that this sure cure, applied to the dying woman on that night of deepest darkness, would chase the pain and restore the spirit of she who was afflicted with the Evil. But, to the great dismay of her kin, the restorative made no difference at all.

Taking her eyes off the awful remedy, little Catharina looked at the familiar arms of her mother that had so often cuddled and comforted her. Now they lay crossed and still upon her breast. A small brass crucifix lay within one porcelain white hand.

"Mama! Wake up, mama!" cried the child after she had kissed the cold face of the silent figure.

"She won't wake up, Catharina," said Little Hans with a soft steady voice. "Mama can't hear you anymore. Come away." He had seen death on the farm; he knew what it meant. Aunt Magdalena swiftly crossed over to the bed, took Catharina from her stricken father, and cradled the girl in her arms.

Looking up at his father, Little Hans asked, "May we leave now?"

The priest, not the father, answered with authority, "Get on your knees, children. We must all pray for the soul of your mother."

And so the small family knelt on the hard wooden floor; they remembered the vitality and love of the good woman; they feared the evil unknown that had taken her from them so suddenly; they implored God to help her in her certain struggle as she languished in purgatory on her journey towards a peaceful eternity; they waited for the night to be over.

CHAPTER THREE

Will the day be bright or cloudy?
Sweetly has its dawn begun.
But the heaven may shake with thunder
'Ere the setting of the sun.

If the wind be fresh and free
The wide skies clear and cloudless blue
The woods and fields and golden flowers
Sparkling in sunshine and in dew
Her days shall pass in Glory's light the world's drear desert through.

—Emily Bronte

JUNE 1505

I.

After the death of his wife, Hans von Bora made the decision to give his daughter a good start in life. At the age of five years, Catharina had been sent to the Benedictine Convent of Brehna near Bitterfeld to be educated in the school and brought up by the good sisters who lived there. However, the

35

tuition proved to be an expense that he could not afford, and after some months, he brought her back to the farm. He loved his daughter; she seemed to bring the sunshine of his wife back to the house; it was good to have her at home again. He would make other plans for his family.

II.

Abundant spring rains had blessed the earth, and it blossomed with great celebration. Purple thistle, white and yellow wild-flowers, and delicate blue forget-me-nots bloomed in carpets of profusion throughout the big meadows of Zulsdorf. Little Hans, Clemons, and Catharina laughed with glee and chased each other in the tall fresh grasses. The birds joined in on the frolic and sang magnificent melodies as they welcomed the beautiful day. Catharina tumbled and landed by a small wild rose growing at the bottom of the hill by the muddy bank of the rushing creek. Hidden from her brothers, she touched its smooth pink petals carefully and rubbed them across her cheek with great pleasure. As the warm breeze gently touched her face, she happily remembered the soft kiss of her mother.

"Hans! Clemons! Catharina! Come quickly to me!" Herr von Bora called from the top of the hill. "Come to the house!"

The children jumped up and ran eagerly to their beloved father. Then they stopped short and grabbed onto each other's hands. He was not alone. Standing next to him was a tall unsmiling woman.

"This is your new mother," the father said. "Her name is Margaret von Ende. She is coming here to live with us, here at our own Zulsdorf."

"Children," said the woman, her voice without emotion in the one-word greeting.

As they looked up at her, all the joy disappeared from their day. Then the woman took the hands of the brothers, but refused that of Catharina.

"Catharina! For shame!" she said sternly as she looked down upon the girl. "Your dress is muddy and dirty with grass stains. And don't you see that you have burrs in your stockings? Pull them off before you enter the house, child. All of them."

The little girl looked at her father. He nodded. As the others disappeared within the farmhouse, Catharina sighed, sat down on the step, and laboriously tried to pick off the stubborn burrs. They were embedded in the stitches of her woolen socks and her skirt. It took her more than an hour to completely remove them one at a time. She missed her noonday meal of sausage, cabbage, and blackened brown bread. It was not kept for her.

CHAPTER FOUR

But Jesus called them unto him, and said, "Suffer little children to come unto me, and forbid them not; for of such is the kingdom of God."

Aber Jesus rief sie zu sich und sprach: "Lasset die Kindlein zu mir kommen und wehret ihnen nicht; denn solcher ist das Reich Gottes."

—Lutherbibel, Lucas 18:16

NOVEMBER 1508

I.

Difficult times faced the Saxon noble families in Lippendorf's province that first decade of the sixteenth century, including that of Hans von Bora. Money and property were concentrated in the pockets and hands of a few ruling families and the Roman Catholic Church. The majority of his neighbors, peasant and highborn alike, worked long hours simply to survive and protect what few acres and possessions they had managed to keep.

Girls were considered a burden upon the purses and hearts of their parents, so marriage provided the only way out of personal poverty. However, betrothal to a man of any material consequence was an impossibility without a substantial dowry. Noble blood was not enough to settle the preconditions of marriage. In addition, unencumbered property together with a sizable sum of money were understood to be dual prerequisites for any union of man and woman. A dim future, indeed, faced the many daughters of Saxony's dwindling and declining nobility whose near-empty pockets could provide neither. Such was the situation for young Catharina von Bora.

Families had more than temporal crises to solve. The fears instilled within them by the Holy Roman Church concerning their spiritual inheritance, duty, and survival also dominated their thinking. According to the tenets of the Church, death did not close the door of guilt and responsibility. Before any man, woman, or child could walk through the everlasting gates of heaven, he or she must linger along the way in a place which the Church called *purgatory.* This was a mandatory and final step of true purification from sin, mandatory unless one was a recognized saint; it was somewhere in an unknown nowhere between earth and heaven, between death and eternal life, apart from God and separated from human life, a place of terrifying nothingness that could last for hundreds or thousands of years, depending upon the weight of the earthly sins committed.

Exit from this dreaded limbo that condemned the dead to a conscious, yet unconscious, survival of spirit could, however, be bought cleanly and legally from the priests for a considerable price. This solution, however, was not available for most. With the weight of purgatory on the minds and hearts of Saxony's fathers, how could they possibly gather together sufficient silver to marry off their young women and still have enough left over to purchase passage out of purgatory for themselves and for beloved grandparents, aunts and uncles, and precious stillborn babies waiting there?

Fortunately, the church did have an answer for these families whose coffers were near empty and whose daughters had no place to go. A holy woman, a nun, had no need for a husband, and, therefore, did not require a sizeable dowry. Furthermore, this course of action would quite conveniently solve more than one problem. In particular, the priests in the local parishes reminded the parents of the admonition of the noted St. Ambrose of Milan to send and keep their daughters unmarried "within the convents, so that through the goodness, purity, and merits of the children, the sins of the parents might be erased." By giving her life to the convent, a young woman could miraculously lessen the pain of purgatory for others.

As a result, mothers and fathers felt duty-bound and somewhat relieved to deposit their dear daughters at the doorstep of one holy order or another. The action was a convenient way to solve some of the problems of both pocketbook and soul in good conscience. Hence, some time after Hans von Bora had temporarily brought little Catharina home from the Benedictine cloister in Brehna, he and his new wife made a more permanent decision in 1508 and transferred her to the strict Cistercian Convent of Nimbschen, near Grimma.

The Cistercians' early eloquent champion was the pious Bernard of Clairveaux, who was known as the Conscience of Christendom. In reaction to the increasing pleasant and liberal convents and monasteries of those in the Benedictine Orders, he "chose the narrowest gate and steepest path to the Kingdom of Heaven." He preached piety, practiced asceticism, and was constantly championing those in poverty while he chastised the rich and powerful. Rather than adopting the black apparel of the Benedictines, the Cistercians wore white with black aprons or veils. In addition to the vows of poverty, obedience, and chastity, they aspired to live a life of constant prayer with the promise to observe silence. There were to be only three reasons for speaking:

spiritual concerns with superiors, necessary work communication, and spontaneous conversation required on special occasions. Many of the women who would spend their lives within the enclosure of the convent would be forgotten as they shed the outside world. Catharina was nine years old.

II.

Hans and Margaret von Bora had stood in the clerical office of the priest of Lippendorf Church. The stepmother of Catharina was obviously quite happy to be there; she had a hopeful and purposeful expression upon her face. The father, however, was uncharacteristically uneasy and looked as if he wished to be elsewhere.

"And, of course," the family priest said, "I urge you to place your little daughter in the Nimbschen Convent. It is a safe and comfortable community for girls of good families such as yours, despite your lack of a fortune."

He paused for a long moment, slowly smiled, and then added, "Particularly–, because of your lack of a fortune. Look at the facts! Your daughter will soon be a young woman. Her childhood is over. It is only realistic to assume that you will not be able to provide an acceptable dowry for a future marriage of consequence. A suitable family or husband will not choose Catharina. The Church in its mercy, however, will exercise its everlasting charity and accept a minimal sum, a very small dowry, as she enters the lifelong security of the convent."

"But what if she is not happy being separated from us?" questioned Hans von Bora. "She is so young, Father. She is devoted to her brothers and dearly loves to come to Zulsdorf. I think that she can still find her mother there."

"She will soon become accustomed to the holy ways as she joyfully embraces her new life," the priest answered as he folded his hands. He stepped closer to the man and looked sternly and steadily into his eyes. After a long pause, he continued, "Hans von Bora! Why do you squirm and hesitate? Do you think only of yourself? What is your decision? Will your daughter have a beautiful life of contemplation and contentment, or will she grow old cleaning pigpens?!"

The father shook his head in quiet despair. The priest continued, "Your child will live a life of constant prayer and will be honored to help in the care of the priceless relics in the Convent Abbey." Silence. An uncomfortable silence. "My son, how can you deny your daughter a serene and well-ordered religious life away from the sinful world?"

"My husband," said the stepmother as she entered the conversation quickly. "Nimbschen is the place for Catharina! We must not stand in the way of such a fine opportunity for our sweet daughter! And we must remember, my dear Herr von Bora, that she will go to the very cloister of your own humble and dedicated dear sister Magdalena! And do not forget that Nimbschen is also under the watchful eye of the Abbess, the honored sister of your gentle departed wife." With folded hands, she added, "God keep her in His arms."

"Two of Catharina's aunts will guide her. But most important, Hans von Bora," concluded the priest with the voice of authority, "her years there within Nimbschen Convent will lessen yours in purgatory. May I also give you the assurance that her commitment will shorten the years of her own mother and your mother— such a good woman she was—in that awful place." He lowered his words to a slow hissing whisper. "Your dead and suffering Catharina von Haubitz has waited long enough in purgatory for you to do something, quite long enough." He paused, waiting for a response from the man.

He got none.

"May God the Father and the Holy Mother and all the saints be with you, guide you, and relieve your consciences," the prelate declared quickly as he blessed the couple with the sign of the cross. The stepmother stepped close to the priest, smiled, and said, "Amen."

The decision was made.

CHAPTER FIVE

Of one that is so fair and bright, brighter than the day is light,
I cry to thee, thou see to me,
Lady, pray thy son for me, that I may come to thee, Maria!
Lady, flow'r of ev'rything,
Thou bare Jesu, Heaven's King.
Of all thou bears the prize, Lady queen of paradise,
Maid mild and Mother.

—medieval melody sung to the Holy Virgin Mary

OCTOBER 8, 1515

I.

"Good morning, Catharina! Wake up! This is the day you have been waiting for!" The voice of Abbess Margarethe was good-natured. Pink streams of dawn filtered into the small cell where the sixteen-year-old novice slept. Morning had come soon and interrupted the deep repose that sometimes descends after hours of tossing and dreaming, resting and reawakening. The young woman sat up, shivered, and pulled her rough linen nightgown around herself. The Abbess closed the window, latched it, and joined her niece in prayer. They both knelt at her bed.

"Holy Father in heaven," Catharina prayed. She tried to stifle a yawn with no success. She was still half asleep.

"Child," said the Abbess firmly, her eyes still closed. "This is not the occasion for irreverence. Begin again."

"Yes, Reverend Mother," Catharina said in embarrassment. "Forgive me." She started a second time. "Dear Jesus in heaven, in all humility I come to you today as your bride. I do not feel very strong, but I am convinced that this is the thing you wish me to do. Help me in my unbelief; pardon me for my many sins of commission and omission; use me as your servant. I pray for the souls of my mother and all my ancestors. I beg you to watch over me on this, my wedding day. In the name of the Father, and the Son, and the Holy Ghost. Amen."

"Amen. Hear us, Lord Jesus," echoed the Abbess. She looked with love at her brother-in-law's only daughter. As she turned to leave Catharina's cell, she said, "Your mother would be so proud of you today. You bless her memory."

"Dear aunt, tell me again. Please tell me again about my mother."

The Abbess hesitated. The sun would not slow down, and there was much yet to be done before the ceremony. Then she laughed with rare tenderness, sat down on the cot and patted it, indicating to Catharina that she should sit down, too. "Yes, my niece. Sometimes I need to talk about her, too." Catharina sat next to the Abbess, quite wide awake now, then searched the face of her aunt and silently waited for any small treasure of remembrance that she could put in her pocket and keep until the times that she needed her mother.

"She was a good woman with far more strength and humility than I have ever been able to muster," said the Abbess. "In our childhood, she would stand up for me and speak out when

I was in trouble, even though I was older than she was. I was quite shy then, would you believe it!"

Catharina smiled, thoroughly enjoying the warmth of her monastic superior, suddenly become Aunt Margarethe, who spoke of the past: "As we were growing up, there were many times that I noticed and profited from her patience. She expected goodness and honorable deeds and, most of all, honesty from others, but she was willing to wait until we thought we had learned it all by ourselves! And, all the time, she taught us by her gentle example."

"What was her voice like?" asked Catharina in an uncharacteristic small whisper. "Sometimes I think I hear her talking to me as she did when I was a very little girl. How did she sound when she spoke?"

The aunt paused. She listened intently to her own memories from long years ago. "Well, her voice was low in pitch, and she played with words like they were a melody." The older woman stared into space, then closed her eyes and shook her head slowly from side to side. After some time, she continued to speak. "If your mother could have been here on this holy day, I think she would tell you what she told me as I was struggling with the decision to enter this convent."

Catharina looked at her aunt in surprise. "Ah, yes, little one, I have not always been so sure of right and wrong. I have had my weaknesses, my doubts. I wanted to come here; my faith in God was absolute, but my faith in myself was lacking. I knew that this life of poverty and unquestioned obedience required a particular inner strength of character if it was to be of any value at all to God and others. And I feared that I did not possess that attribute." She paused a moment, well aware that she was about to share, yea, to give Catharina priceless and remarkable words of wisdom from the girl's own dead mother—words that she herself had treasured and privately whispered time and time and time again during her long and lonely years at the convent.

"As well as I remember, my child, these were your mother's

words to me: 'Before anything can truly become part of your character, my sister, you must permit it; you must be still and think about it. We weave character as a spider weaves at his entrance; we weave it and cut it and sew it and wear it. You have the making of a sculpture, and, oh, the good that you can do!'"

They sat together silently for a few moments side by side, each full of thoughts and thanks for the wisdom and the life of the first Catharina von Bora. The trappings and duties and responsibilities of the Cistercian order were forgotten, even invisible. Bathed in the serenity that comes from wholeness, they sat there together. Then, the Abbess, suddenly remembering her station at Nimbschen Convent, returned to the present, got to her feet, cleared her throat which had become rather husky, and once again assumed her position as Mother Superior.

The Abbess fussed with the door handle longer than necessary. "And now, dwell on your sinful nature, Catharina," she said with authority, turning around. "Your humility, your good deeds, and pure life will one day earn your presence in heaven. God be with you, my dear niece." Abbess, not aunt, Margarethe von Haubitz withdrew into the hallway in haste and shut the door.

II.

Catharina had completed all the requirements for taking her final vows for Sisterhood of the Cloister. Of greatest personal importance to her was finding a reason for each day given to her by God. This hope was fulfilled, but not often enough, by her studies. She learned to read, both in her mother tongue and, less fluently, in Latin; the beautifully scripted letters of the two languages were constantly a source of satisfaction, for she had a keen mind and truly loved to learn. The young nuns were instructed in some church history and read a bit about theology in their own language, as approved by a few visiting professors and priests from German universities. The convent owned a small library of books that had been printed on Gutenberg's printing presses; these leather-bound tomes were treasures closely akin in value to some of the relics in the Abbey. Any looking at or paging through the Holy Bible, of course, was not permitted, but the priests read aloud from it on occasion—only in Latin—for that book had never been translated into the common vernacular. And as months and years passed, the sisters worshiped at hundreds of matins, masses, vespers, and prayers where they heard the Psalms from the Old Testament over and over again. Catharina memorized many of them. The Latin language was still extremely foreign to her, but the verses were tantalizing enough for her to learn to love them and desire to read them—Psalm 31, in particular. But reading the beloved Psalms was not possible. Only the ordained clergy read from the Scriptures, not the nuns. In fact, Catharina did not expect to ever hold the holy book in her own hands.

All the novices were required to prove their humility by spending long hours in menial tasks. As her nine-year-old niece grew into a strong young woman, the Abbess had watched with satisfaction as Catharina became a diligent and efficient worker in the convent gardens. The truth, however, was that Catharina felt the sunny hours of the growing season slip by blissfully unnoticed when she could spend them observing and nurturing the plants. Sometimes, impatient for the seeds to develop into tiny flowers or vegetables, she dug down to inspect them and cried a tear or two and asked forgiveness if she accidentally broke off a fragile stem. "Next time," she promised herself, "next time, I will have more patience. I will wait!"

From beyond the garden perimeter, the Abbess carefully watched the girl's concentration and diligence with satisfaction, but she saw more than that. Pulling memories from her own childhood, she relived the many times that she and Catharina's mother, her little sister, spent long hours working on the farm of their father. She could see the fir wilderness that encircled the fields and smell the pungent floor of damp pine needles, a foot or two deep in some places on the forest floor. The trees were home to hundreds of glorious songbirds; she and her sister knew every song, knew and befriended every bird that sang them. Now, so many years later, her sister was no more on this earth, but, as if by a sacred miracle sent directly from God, there she was again talking to the flowers, singing back to the birds, and pulling stubborn weeds from the hard soil—in the person of her sister's young daughter. The two Catharinas often merged for the Abbess, until she chided herself in strong terms for welcoming personal and selfish pleasure when she should be concentrating on the eternal world, not this evil one.

The gardening was not all joy for Catharina, however; it was often a source of some of her chronic problems. Yes, she was guilty. She broke The Silence knowingly while talking to the cabbages. She further degraded it by humming melodies under her breath as she planted and hoed. There would be no evening supper on those nights. More than once, a hungry Catharina recalled other such nights back at Zulsdorf when her new step-mother used the same measures for breaking rules. She survived as a little girl; she would survive now. Additionally, on far too many occasions, she rushed to prayers from the gardens only to have black soil discovered underneath her fingernails. Dirty folded hands were not to be tolerated! Stern reprimands were accepted, but not always remembered the next day. The ado about fingernails simply made no sense! Young Catharina was convinced that the dirt out there in the garden and only slightly misplaced beneath her nails was quite wonderful! It was far different and much more acceptable than the dirt and leaves that constantly collected inside the drafty ancient buildings. As punishment for her carelessness, Catharina wore down many a broom as she swept clouds of renegade dust out of the rooms, down the stone steps, and back onto the ground where it was supposed to have stayed in the first place.

"Sister Catharina! Silence! You talk too much! You even think

50

with a loud voice!" Yes, another constant example of the young nun's sin was her tongue. Catharina had a way of speaking at the most inopportune times—before she thought. Her ideas often clashed with those of authority, and she found it almost impossibly difficult to keep her opinions to herself. The girl scrubbed many mossy cellar walls to atone for her verbal transgressions.

Nevertheless, after years of trial and error, sin and forgiveness, learning well and growing up, Catharina von Bora the novice was accepted for inclusion by the convent community, and she prepared to take her final vows at Nimbschen Convent. She was convinced that she was more than ready for the new significance in her life that this day would certainly bring.

III.

Three hours after being awakened, Catharina stood an arm's length from Ave and Margarethe Schoenfeld at the door of the Abbey. The two sisters were ready to make their permanent promises alongside Catharina. They were girls of uncommon beauty with dark blue eyes, dark eyebrows finely drawn, and clear skin unmarked by scars of disease. And, unusual for German females, their teeth were complete, white, and even. The three did not touch hands, nor did they speak to each other. Eyes downcast, each was alone, as it should be.

The families and friends of the girls, together with the entire religious community, had been invited to gather together in the pews to observe the ceremonies as the virginal novices became brides of the Church. Hundreds of holy candles on the twelve altars lit the interior of the old Abbey. The heavy smell of wax, smoke, and incense mingled with the dampness from the old stone walls and floor of the church.

Catharina knew that the next steps she would take down the familiar aisle of the Abbey could not be retraced without personal eternal consequences that she alone must face. She shivered. Out of nowhere, oppressive doubt flooded her being. "I don't want to be by myself anymore," she thought to herself in silent desperation. "Oh, papa, take me home to my birds and wildflowers, to my own little bed!" For a frantic moment, solitude seemed senseless when her beloved family was so close. Her eyes lifted, and she discreetly searched the congregation gathered there for a sight of her father and brothers, but she could not find them. She knew they were there, somewhere; she needed to see them and be assured that they were happy for her.

In disappointment, her glance wandered and fell upon the last row of worshipers where a family with three children sat closely crowded together. The mother held a very small girl whose sunlit blonde tousled curls could not be tamed beneath her white lace cap. The eyes of the child, peeking from behind her mother's shoulder, fixed upon Catharina who stood only a few feet away. As the dimpled little one smiled at her with sparkling expectation, Catharina, without warning, felt another painful tug deep within her. "I will never have children," she whispered silently to herself. This was no new revelation, of course. For several years she had been told and sincerely accepted this fact—a husband and giving birth to a child was never to be part of her life. Indeed, it was her gift to God to turn her back on such thoughts. As she looked back at the little girl, the cold and certain reality of her decision became a heavy aching burden for which there would be no answer, no relief. But the choice had been made. "Is it not better that I please God, that I offer my life to the poor, that I leave no worry for my dear father?" she cried deep within her soul. One, just one small tear fell; Catharina quickly looked away from the child, brushed the wayward tear from her face, asked God's forgiveness for her weakness, and with determination she stood tall and stared straight ahead down the aisle towards the great carved altar where her future beckoned.

The nuns' chorus sang a lengthy antiphonal psalmody only

slightly off-key before the service began. As their pitch gradually dipped from a half step flat to even a bit more, the choral leader of the choir struck a tuning fork with a silver mallet, and the group obediently raised its pitch to the proper key for a few minutes until it began to sink again, only to be prompted upward by the persistent mallet. Finally, the singing was over, and the three young women were led to the front of the congregation by a procession of priests wearing elaborately embroidered vestments. The nuns' choir sang a two hundred year-old hymn to the Virgin.

Catharina, garbed in a simple white dress and opaque veil, stood quietly as she awaited her turn to be accepted into the order.

IV.

When the rites had been completed for Margarethe and Ave, Catharina was taken to the center of the aisle before the grand central altar. She lay down on the cold granite flagstones, her face pressed to the floor and her arms outstretched so that her body formed the shape of a cross.

> Lord, have mercy upon us.
> Holy, Holy, Holy Lord God of Hosts,
> Heaven and earth are full of Thy Glory.
> O Lamb of God, who takest away the sins of the world,
> Have mercy upon us.
> Grant us peace.

After the words of institution by the presiding bishop and as he administered the Eucharist to her immediate family, she felt the hand of her dear aunt, Magdalena, the jolly and comfortable sister of her father, the nun she had chosen to present her to her

Heavenly Bridegroom. The threefold Kyrie Eleison rang again through all the dusty sunlit cubicles and niches of the Abbey. "Lord, have mercy upon us. Christ, have mercy upon us. Lord, have mercy upon us."

The Kyrie echoed into expectant stillness. Sister Magdalena raised up Catharina and removed the simple bridal veil, took a pair of sharp shears from her habit pocket, and carefully cut off the girl's heavy brown tresses. Her head bowed, Catharina saw her hair fall on the floor in disarray. At that moment, she remembered her beloved mother's death pillow and the picture, never to be forgotten, of the loose brown hair framing her cold countenance. Catharina raised her head and sought the eyes of her father. There he was sitting only a few yards away! "Papa, papa, I love you!" she called in silence. He looked at her with tears daring to cover his cheeks. Both of them knew that the monumental invisible barrier, now forever between them, would never be stronger than their compassion for one another.

Catharina then took her vows, life-changing words of obedience, chastity, poverty, and life-long commitment. She gave the rest of her days to contemplation and prayer within the enclosure of the convent walls, content to be forgotten by the world except for hours spent in service to the weary, hungry, and sick.

A priest intoned the creed of the Christian church while two of the older nuns approached Catharina.

Credo in unum Deum, Patrem omnipotentum,
Factorem coeli et terrae, visibilium omniuim et invisibilium.
Credo in unum Domininum Iesum Christum, Filium Dei
    unigenitum,
Et ex Patre natum ante omnia saecula.
Deum de Deo; lumen de Lumine;
Deum verum de Deo vero; genitum non factum;
Consubstantialem Patri, per quem omnia facia sunt.
Qui propter nos homines,
et propter nostram salutem, descendit de coelis,

Et incarnatus est de Spritu Sancto ex Maria Virgine, et
homo factus est.

The priest continued glorifying God with his beautiful bari-
tone voice as the elder sisters pulled a new white garment over
Catharina's head. It had been made sacred by incense, prayers,
and sprinkling of holy water. They wound a black rope girdle
around her waist and placed a black veil on her head. Then
the Abbess herself set a wreath of white roses upon Catharina's
forehead as she became the Bride of Heaven. The teacher of the
novices pressed a crucifix carved of olive wood from Bethlehem
into her hands. It would be her sole possession. They all stepped
away, and she stood alone before the altar.

... Et expecto Resurrectionem mortuorum et venturi sacculi.
Amen.

V.

Catharina had observed this ceremony several times before in
the seven years that she had lived at the convent. Now, she
was the one who stood there, so close to the Presence of the Most
High God and in the paternal shadow of the powerful Church
of Rome. She again became aware and fearful of her many
human frailties and felt not at all certain to be worthy of the
white roses, of the sacred life which stretched out before her. As
Catharina removed the wreath of fragrant flowers and offered it
to her Bridegroom, her fingers brushed the softness of the petals,
so much like the small pink ones covering the hillsides of Zulsdorf
in the hot summertime. She would not return there now, save for
dire family emergency. "It is time to set that life aside," she scolded
herself. "I now belong to my Lord." She set the crown of blossoms
upon the altar and suddenly thought of the fierce thorns that

had composed His crown. "Wear my roses, Jesus," she whispered so that nobody could hear. "There have been too many thorns."

Catharina turned and walked to a small ornately carved table at the side of the altar. On it was a small red velvet pouch. She picked it up with trembling hands. The great quiet of the old church hung over her; she retraced her steps to the altar; the sound of her own shoes echoed to the very last row of the nave. Catharina untied the strings of the bag and poured its contents of coins into a silver vessel. It was her dowry. Thirty groats—all that her father could afford. She felt his eyes upon her and wished for his steady arm around her shoulders.

The coins clanged noisily into the offering receptacle. The new nun turned and walked down the seven steps to the spot where the Abbess stood. She knelt at the feet of her aunt and vowed obedience to the Cistercian Sisters for all eternity. As she rose, the entire congregation, nuns and monks and priests and lay people alike, joined her; by rising, they welcomed and received her as a blessed bride.

All those assembled continued to stand for another hour while the priests completed the mass from the altar and from the pulpit that perched high above the people. To her distress, Catharina erred a good deal even on this her holiest of days; she kept reaching for understanding of each spoken and chanted Latin word, chided herself for lack of patience and thinking only of herself, and prayed for God's forgiveness. Then, in disappointment, she caught herself trying to translate again. "I shall never gain true humility," she thought as she struggled to achieve the serenity expected of her new position in the Church. "But I will try. Lord, have mercy upon me."

"Glory be to God on high, and on earth peace, good will towards men," chanted the priests just as they and their predecessors had sung for centuries in the same ancient melody. "We praise thee, we bless thee, we worship thee, we glorify thee, we give thanks to thee for thy great glory, O Lord God, heavenly King, God the Father Almighty. O Lord, the only begotten Son,

Jesus Christ; O Lord God, Lamb of God, Son of the Father, that takest away the sins of the world, have mercy upon us."

Sister Catharina and all the others closed the service in unison:

Amen, Amen, Amen.

CHAPTER SIX

Jog on, Jog on, the footpath way
And merrily hent the stile-a:
A merry heart goes all the day,
Your sad tires in a mile-a.

—William Shakespeare, The Winter's Tale, Act 4, Scene 2

1520

To walk awhile in the days of Catharina von Bora and to attempt to understand the lives of her contemporaries, we must cross their thresholds, wander on their footpaths, taste their gruel, respect their medieval fears, and honor their struggle for survival. It is easy to dwell upon the dreadful omens and superstitions, the poverty, ignorance, and pain. But that was not the sum of their lives. There was laughter and worry, forgiveness and revenge, yes, even contentment as well as greed. The smile of a child born in any century can erase the clouds of despair.

The sad mystery of history is that it so often evokes boredom and a yawn. The people who walked upon this earth are often shrouded in the fog of the years. This is impossible when the past is made as real as the present. These ancestors of modern man laughed and they cried; they worked by day and slept by night; they hurt when they stumbled on stones, and they were feverish when sick; they trusted that the sun would rise the next morning.

Yes, life in the sixteenth century was hard, fearsome, and wearying. But did not the Church declare Sunday to be a day of rest, a day to stop the toil and concentrate on the sacred, a day to take the time to listen to the commands of the holy fathers? It was also a common practice that the country folk, including the women, were given permission to hold their feasts and fairs as they attended the religious festivals. Even so, farmers could not always obey the priests; the skies, the rain, the cold, the sleet, and the winds held precedence over a bishop.

There are times when the daily drudgery of simple survival requires a respite—a bit of humor and some hours of fun and festivity. So it was with the Saxon folk. All was not doom and gloom, disease and death, and fear of the unknown.

Every village had its patron saint and thus his or her festival day. The Church allowed and celebrated over twenty such anniversaries that were often combined with a village fair. On these religious holidays, a flag was flown from the spire of the church, and the days were considered free days for the peasants. Together, the holy days plus the fair provided the chance for the populace to come together for both sacramental and secular events. A parade of peasants through the town often opened the gaiety; they carried and clanged household utensils with ladles, waved brooms high in the air, wore barrels on their heads as they stumbled down the paths to the delight of all, and carried flute players on their shoulders. The Church frowned on the boisterous behavior that often ruled the day and was loudly exhibited. Sermons were preached against it, but, nevertheless, the priests also took part in the merrymaking and revelry. These holidays helped to satisfy a part of the evolving national and personal pride in the movement for some freedom and independence. Printed broadsheets, scattered about in prominent public places, even dared to anonymously criticize the clergy and painted their holiday behavior as avarice, false worship, and hypocrisy.

Weddings often took place on these festival days. Traditionally, the sacrament had been administered outside at the front door of the church. It wasn't until 1525 that Lutheran pastors in Nuremberg celebrated the weddings within the church before the altar. The sacrament of marriage followed both religious and local regulations. The serf paid his lord a marriage tax and required his permission to marry. This tax was often as much as the cost to buy a small house. Property, not love, was the first consideration. Betrothal was as binding and permanent as was the marriage. The couples knew that their future would probably include the lifelong work of raising ten to fifteen sons and daughters including, as a matter of course and acceptance, any illegitimate children. As a result, when all considerations had been met, the wedding day was celebrated as a "rare moment of joy" with hours of drinking and dancing. The couple and their friends often consumed a gallon of wine apiece on this special day and frolicked the hours away. Hans Sachs, the leading poet of Nuremberg wrote:

> The wine was knocked back so hastily
> That many of them fell under the bench,
> They also raised a great clamor of spitting,
> Shouting, screaming, singing, and crying.

City regulations together with the Church considered dancing as immoral, on paper. In truth, all the levels of society took part in it.

> There's naught more evil here on earth
> than giddy dancing, gaily done

at Kermes, first mass, where the fun
is shared by priests and laity.

It was not difficult to identify the social stratas. The middle and upper classes, dressed in their heavily embroidered lavish clothing, looked down upon the peasants as stupid, rude, and naïve people who possessed no proper social conduct. Woodcuts from the time illustrate that their aristocratic dances were popular. On a typical holiday, known as the Kirchweith, the rich heartily enjoyed the action but prided themselves in restraint with courtly, sedate, and pleasant dances.

On the other hand, the peasants exhibited questionable behavior, even throwing girls up into the air so that their legs showed! The men wore pants, blouses, boots, and felt hats, while all the maidens wore kerchiefs tied under their chins. Their behavior and table manners were scorned; spoons and forks were not to be seen. Food was eaten with the fingers. "God would not have given us fingers if he wanted us to use forks," declared one priest who eagerly joined in on the gaiety.

A charming dance for all classes was called Row Dancing in which the woman wore garlands of flowers or leaves in a circlet upon her hair, and her partner stuck the flowers in his hatband. During the dance, the couples followed each other in a circle as onlookers sang or played lilting tunes. A less pleasing dance was the Nose Dance. Folks in the area known for their distinctive noses danced in a ring, pulling each other's noses. Sachs again commented:

Peasants and their relatives came running up,
An enormous multitude all provided with long noses
Long, fat, and bent, droopy and pocked.
Crooked, snotty, broad, plump, and spotty,
Pointed, broken, and lumpy,
Wormy, woody, and knotty.

The competitor with the largest nose won a garland while second place received a nose sock to use in frosty weather. Third place walked away with a pair of underpants. This was one of the most popular activities at the fair/church "holy days"!

These holidays were also a grand time to conduct local business, since they were about the only times that people from the town and surrounding areas, city residents and farmers alike, would get together. The peasants brought cartfuls of produce, fish, and fowl to sell. Cloth, leather goods, and jewelry were hawked beneath the trees and upon the stone fences. With a few coins, the women could purchase shiny colorful ribbons as well as handmade lace to decorate their braids, collars, aprons, and caps. The professional set also took advantage of the crowded roads and plied their trades wherever they could find a spot to be seen. They were not all legitimate honorable tradesmen. Dentists were known to seat a poor man with a painful tooth upon a tree stump and yank out the tooth with a huge pair of pliers. As the man howled in pain, the dentist's accomplice deftly removed any coins from the patient's back pockets. This practice was common enough to be etched in several existing woodcuts.

There is nothing like competition to raise the spirits, talents, and voices! The fair was the noisy scene of games of skill for all classes and ages. Barefoot men leaped over sword blades while they balanced glasses on their heads. Avoiding chickens scratching in the dirt and pigs eating pilfered cabbages, the folks played games of ninepins and raced their horses. With their long skirts billowing behind them, women ran in foot races, while children wrestled each other and searched for money lost on the ground during the merriment.

Revelry, too much drink, and inattention among the citizens provided an obvious opportunity for thieves. Some were simple peasants who artfully supported themselves and a life of idleness by unobtrusively mingling with the fairgoers and pocketing a few bangles and coins. But ominous danger also lurked. Unemployed roaming mercenaries known as the Landsknechte

were known to wreak havoc by plundering churches and loot-
ing other public property; the festival and the purses of the peasants and highborn alike were no exception, so most men had a
weapon of some sort tucked within their clothing.

The festival days provided some misery for women without a husband. A woman born in Saxony in the 1500's was
expected to marry at a young age, bring a dowry and loyalty
and goodness to her husband's family, produce healthy children,
and obediently work side-by-side with her husband. In fact, a
16th century German proverb declared the common sentiment
concerning dominating females: "A bad woman is three times
worse than the devil. A devoted wife is worth more than her
weight in gold." A single woman might join the nuns in a convent; this was considered an appropriate and honorable way of
life. If she did not enter a religious order or was not chosen to be a
bride for one reason or another, she shamed both herself and her
family. At the village fair, unmarried women of all ages who
had no suitors were forced to pull a plow around the boundaries
of the town like a team of oxen while onlookers mocked and
jeered them. On the other hand, an old German engraving gave
advice to men and praised a happy marriage:

Take a wife.
God determines how your life together will be.
Stay with her in love and suffering and always be patient.
And if you should have much worry and care,
Look on it as God's will.
Provide for her by the sweat of your brow
As God commanded in the first book of Genesis.

Both husband and wife should know their place.

Go ahead and act like a man!
Otherwise she'll end up riding you,
And before long she'll

Deprive you of your pants, your purse, and your sword.
Which will make us all ashamed of you.
Do not give her too much rein,
But rather take an oak cudgel
And beat her soundly between the ears!

And so the festival days displayed many unadorned facets
of the times, good and bad, unruly and charming. Even as the
populace used the holidays for brawling, bedlam, and good honest fun, the Church steeple was always a towering presence. The
folks went home; the celebration receded in memory. The Church
remained, and its authority was inescapable.

Chapter Seven

"If we look back upon the nineteen centuries of Christianity, with all their heroes, kings, and saints, we shall find it difficult to list many who came so close to Christian perfection as the nuns. Their lives of quiet devotion and cheerful ministration have made many generations blessed."

—Will Durant, The Age of Faith

Spring and Summer of 1517

I.

As the tidal wave of enormous religious controversy and social change swept across the forests and fields of sixteenth century Germany, the strong and steady force reached even into the gardens and recesses of the venerable convent at Grimma. The walls of invincible isolation were impenetrable no longer. The fortress would seriously begin to crumble when Martin

Luther's writings and, later, his translations of the New Testament, would pass in through the windows of the Nimbschen Abbey and into the hands and hearts of pious women who could read.

It all began on a chilly spring day in northeast Saxony, the kind of day when the winds pierced through the worn coats of the peasants. It was a bone-chilling unrelenting sunshine that spread across the hills. The crusty dirty snow had melted, and it was time to start the plowing of the gardens and fields and to begin seeding with the supply carefully saved from the best part of last autumn's harvest. But the people were not thinking of farming. The relief from winter that the birth of spring would normally bring had been supplanted by a dreadful fear this year—terror of a horrible and deadly sickness that indiscriminately and swiftly struck wealthy prince and poor washerwoman, aged grandfather and two-year-old baby, saint and sinner. The merciless hand of Death had opened many a door, taken its quarry, and left quickly, only to return again and again. Infant mortality was high, and countless new mothers also perished with complications of birth, the unknown illness, vermin, and ignorance. Sometimes called "distemper," the often-fatal malady defied all known medicines. For the first few days, a high and violent fever raged within the victims; hence, the name, "sweating sickness." Another tortuous and intolerably painful symptom was the appearance of large stone-hard purplish-black swellings and putrid boils, usually on the neck or legs. If these were lanced successfully, somehow avoiding fatal infection from filthy medical knives or, as a last resort, red-hot iron implements, the patient had a chance for recovery. More often than not, the treatment was as deadly as the disease and hastened the end, and life was cruelly snuffed out. A tall red cross painted on the door of every house visited by Death declared untold agony; above it the words "Lord have mercy upon us" were hastily scrawled in big letters.

Astrologers added to the panic and had more than ordinary influence upon the minds of the common people. They watched the night skies religiously and saw the dreadful judgment of the heavens in the movement of the stars. Sounds of thunder from above were suspected to carry the Death into one's body through the ears; therefore, the dreaded onset of the approaching April rainstorms added to the fear of each new day. The terrified folks believed in the omens, saw apparitions in the air, and heard voices warning them of God's anger. Furthermore, it was an accepted fact that if the demons of the underworld so chose, they could frighten a man to death on the eve of no moon, even though he had avoided the sickness.

At the height of the horror, some districts required that the corpse-laden carts would travel to the burying place only between sunset and sunrise. Town authorities hoped to hide the extent of the pestilence. As the drivers gathered the dead and passed through the streets, cries of women and children at their windows were the only funeral dirge. Then, following a revolutionary practice begun in France in an attempt to halt the onslaught of the plague, those afflicted in Saxony and neighboring principalities were isolated in their houses or hovels for forty days, quarantined from all others except for visitations of charity from monastics of nearby holy orders.

As persistence of the virulent epidemic finally began to wane, Abbess Margarethe of Nimbschen Convent felt conditions were safe enough to send some of her nuns who were skilled in the practice of nursing to the stricken village of Jüterbog. It was not many miles from Wittenberg and just across the Saxon border. So it happened that on a chilly spring morning shortly before dawn, Sister Magdalena, Sister Catharina, and a few other Cistercian women arrived to aid the suffering people. The year was 1517.

II.

"Welcome to Jüterbog," said the weary but relieved priest who met them at the steps of the church. Wrapped in a heavy black cape, he was an old man of nearly sixty years and did not appear to be in good health himself. His sparse graying hair and wrinkled face were very nearly the same ashen hue. He coughed and spat from deep within his chest, then spoke slowly. "We are most grateful that you are here. Was your journey difficult? You must be very cold."

"Thank you for your concern, Father," replied Sister Magdalena, speaking for the others as she stepped unsteadily from the wagon that had carried them northward. "Yes, four days in the chill of the open air gave us pains in our knees that we never had before." She rubbed a deep ache in her back and slowly straightened up. "But we slept well with good folk in Torgau and Würzen and in a warm dry inn near Herzberg. We are most anxious to help your people in any way we can."

"The devil and his armies have been hard at work here in our village," the priest said sadly. "The sickness has left no home untouched; scores are already dead; many more are dying. Ah, the cries of the little ones are heard everywhere! Some children cry because they are very sick. Others have lost their mothers and fathers. They do not understand. I do think that the fear is almost worse than the pest itself—for all of us." Pausing, his words hung in the cold air. He continued, "Grown children have left their dying parents to care for themselves, hoping to fly away from the disease. Old men and women suffer and die alone. I must admit that I dare not go to their bedsides; I can only offer the sacrament over their graves." Salty tears filled his eyes; he could finally speak to someone, to spiritual comrades, about his ordeal of lonely frustration and inability to administer the sacraments properly in the eyes of the Church. The relief permitted release of emotion long withheld from public view. He wept. Then, in control again, he said, "Thank you, thank you, dear sisters, for coming to us." He coughed, and spat into the snow.

"Yes, yes," murmured Sister Magdalena who understood exactly what he was trying to say. She rescued him from the moment and took charge of the situation. "But we did not travel

70

all this way to talk on the church steps! Show us where to go."
Not one to waste time, she looked up at the nuns still in the
wagon. "Come, sisters! Gather up your baskets and bundles! We
have much work to do!"

The priest first led the group to the home of a prosperous
lawyer, Herr Peter Hochstetter, who had lost his entire family
to the pestilence—wife, two sons barely grown into manhood,
father, and great-aunt. Neither gold in his strongbox nor a well-
stocked larder nor high position in the courts were a smidgeon
of value as the hand of Death came slinking into his home. Full
of grief, he retreated to the solace of his books and pen and
offered his home as a hospital of sorts for some of the deserted
souls who had been left to perish alone. The gabled house was
three stories high; the ground floor provided commodious space
for the workplace and library of the jurist and also, in the back,
the living quarters for the servants. The family had lived above
where many windows with polished glass panes filled the rooms
with sunlight. The dwelling was warm. Four large stoves faced
with delicately designed ceramic tiles reflected the heat. Plentiful
cords of wood from nearby forests, stored in a shed behind the
building, were sufficient for one more winter. Beautifully made
coats lined with fur, shirts fashioned of colorful silk, feathered
hats, yards of costly lace, buckled shoes, and soft satin slippers
embroidered with pearls and ribbons filled chests and cupboards.
There was nobody left to wear them.

III.

It was to this house of abundance and shadows that the nuns went
with their poultices, their energy, their care, and their prayers. But
the priest soon took Sisters Magdalena and Catharina aside. "I
need you elsewhere," he whispered. Asking no questions, they
bade the others good-bye, turned, and followed him back out

into the chilly air. Without explanation, he walked ahead of the two women through the narrow cobbled streets, deserted except for several scurrying rats. He led them to the local cemetery.

The sacred ground, the earthly resting place of generations of Jüterbog's families, was marked with the oldest graves near to the gate. The old priest made his way through the maze of names, crosses, and mossy inscriptions. Without thinking, he avoided stepping on an occasional eager green shoot pushing itself through last November's dead weeds and leaves. At the edge of the older section of the cemetery, he stopped. The two women, their cloaks flapping in the bitter wind, were close behind. The reality of the town's disaster stared at them, for straight ahead they saw the somber results of a winter of death. Mound after mound of freshly turned earth, some already starting to settle into the ground, rose in mute orderly obeisance to the sickness and covered the defenseless dead.

The priest said to the nuns, "Stop here. Go no further." He pointed to the far corner of the graveyard. Two figures struggled with shovels as they tried to dig into the barely thawed earth. Catharina noticed immediately that one of them, a woman, heavy with child, was struggling to stand. Catharina looked quickly at the priest and said, "We must help her!" She impulsively started towards the pregnant woman. "No!" ordered the priest; he grabbed her arm and drew her back. She looked at him in disbelief. "Father, the woman is in trouble! We must go to her!"

"Sister Catharina! You forget yourself," Magdalena whispered loudly.

"But, . . ." began Catharina.

"You cannot go to them," said the priest. "They must do the work themselves. You dare not go any closer!"

The peasant woman groaned and leaned against her shovel. Again, Catharina implored the priest. "Good Father, I must help her. Why do you stop me?"

"You will have the chance to aid the poor soul," he answered. "But not yet, Sister. You do not understand. When a child dies, only the parents can dig the grave in the far far corner of the cemetery and bury him themselves. Not one gravedigger in the town will get close to the body. The dread of the disease is too great." He leaned close to the women. "Listen carefully, sisters. We hear strange rumors that one who touches or even looks upon the dead child will somehow, in some way, be afflicted also. The spirit of the sickness rises from the corpse and attacks the living! Surely, you have heard this in Grimma. You understand, that is why I cannot be part of the burial! We are convinced this is scientific truth! No citizen here would ever call for a doctor. Rather, we feel we must run away from them because they most certainly are full of the evil. They have held the hands of the dead! And so, the parents here in Jüterbog have been burying their own children." Deep wretched coughing stopped his speech. He sighed, "Only a week ago, these two laid their two daughters in the ground. Today, they bury their firstborn, their only son. He was only seven years old. He died at the break of dawn today. Wait, Sister Catharina, wait until the soil has covered the boy; then it should be safe for you and good Sister Magdalena to go to their house and aid with the birth of the newborn baby. You do see the good sense in treading carefully around the pest, don't you?"

Tears fell from Catharina's eyes. The cold gusts of wind blew them across her cheeks. No, she did not understand! There was so much misery in the world. With the help of God and within the sanction of the Church, she desperately wanted to make a difference. But even this ordained priest of Rome was afraid! Her hands trembled beneath her cloak, first, because of the penetrating cold and, even more, because of her anger towards the great unknown powers of disease and devils that could destroy a good family in just one week. How could she and her aunt, who were so limited in their knowledge of anything beyond the walls of Nimbschen Convent, combat so fierce an enemy with only their baskets of bandages and brown bread and simple remedies for weapons?

Catharina would never forget the sight of those two grieving parents shoveling, stopping, sighing, then digging again down, down, into the rocky stubborn earth. Finally, the father took the shovel from his wife and gently sat her beside the small body of their boy, wrapped in his own gray goat hair blanket. With one hand on his still form and her other upon her own swelling stomach, the mother wept and whispered, "My little unborn one, say good-bye to your brother." The wind carried her sobbing words to the three watchers who stood in silence. Catharina and Magdalena cried unashamedly.

It was time. But the mother was not ready to release her beloved child. The old priest gasped in horror as she drew aside the blanket and kissed the dead boy's face. After rememorizing every feature, she covered him. The father helped her to her feet, and the two of them lifted their son, all wrapped in gray, and laid him in his cold lonely bed of German soil. The mother turned away, leaned heavily against the trunk of a huge tree, and pressed her face into its rough bark while the stonefaced father spaded the earth back into the grave. "You are his mother now, great tree," she sobbed. "Watch over him; he fears the dark."

"She has kissed the face of the dead," the priest whispered loudly to the two nuns. "She will surely be next! And if you touch her, you will be victims in short order. I release you from this task of mercy; you may return to the house of Herr Hochstetter and work with the others."

Sister Magdalena looked at her niece who shook her head in disagreement. "No, Father," she said in a firm voice to the priest. "No. We are here for mercy's sake and here we will stay."

IV.

An hour later, they entered the lowly hut of the weary peasants. The priest did not go inside, but blessed the door of the home with words from Psalm 91, which he had cried to the heavens before many dwellings. "I will say of the Lord, He is my refuge and my fortress: my God; in him will I trust. Surely he shall deliver thee from the snare of the fowler, and from the noisome pestilence. Thou shalt not be afraid for the terror by night; nor for the arrow that flieth by day; Nor for the pestilence that walketh in darkness; nor for the destruction that wasteth at noon day." His voice rose. "A thousand shall fall at thy side, and ten thousand at thy right hand; but it shall not come nigh thee. There shall no evil befall thee, neither shall any plague come nigh thy dwelling." His arms reaching and pleading heavenward, the old priest called for the damnation of the unnatural spirits within. He bid the nuns good-bye. As he hurried away, he looked back at the thatched roof of the hut and saw rats with twitching tails watching him. He cursed the scurrying creatures and then went his way, returning to his own modest lodging and common-law wife.

V.

It was a humble house. The two nuns followed the man and woman and stepped over the threshold; inside, the very walls seemed to moan with overwhelming sorrow. Some light from the outdoors filtered through the dingy oiled paper panes that fit into the small window frames. The paper, cracked and torn in some places, kept the winter out and the smoke within during the long cold months of October through March. Over in the corner of the first room known as the main room, Catharina saw that the fire was almost out. A few scattered embers glowed in the darkness of the hearth. It was built at floor level with stone and plaster oven walls rising around it and a wide-spaced grill above which provided the cooking surface. Hanging over the ashes was a large iron pot. A few pieces of kindling and three or four birch logs were stacked by the wall. The floor, constructed of large uneven flagstones around the fire and hard scraped dirt elsewhere was almost hidden by straw, which in turn was covered by woven hemp mats. More loose straw was pushed into cracks between the floor and the walls to insulate against the weather. Additional piles of hay were scattered about the floor; they provided a little extra warmth for the family's feet. A long wooden table strewn with several unwashed eating utensils in disarray, two benches, a near-empty vegetable barrel, a tall oak chest with carvings on each drawer, and two beds with rumpled bedding—one long, one short—comprised the furniture. High on the walls, three shelves held some tarnished metal plates, a few pewter bowls, some earthenware pots, cooking kettles, and an iron candlestick. There were wooden pegs for clothing; on them hung three threadbare coats, the size that children would wear, a dark green shawl with knotted fringes, and a small wool cap. Catharina looked up towards the dimly-lit ceiling and shuddered. In the corners and across the beams, she saw dusty masses of thickly strung spider webs, full of eggs. A doorway led to a small room; it was a sleeping chamber furnished with another low bed and a stool.

The spider webs did not last very long. After taking a hasty survey about the place, Magdalena went into action.

"Sister Catharina," she began. "I will tend to the good woman. Her child will be born very soon, I fear. But she needs food; she has no strength left. The first thing you must do is throw out the mess of pottage and begin anew." The pregnant woman looked at Sister Magdalena as if she was about to commit a mortal sin. "It is all right, my little mother," soothed the nun. "It's almost Lent. The angels will look the other way. It is time to clean the pot."

As in most cottages and modest homes, the soup kettle was scrubbed out but once a year with great ceremony and blessings from the priest—and only at the onset of Lent. Using salted fish or, if times were fortunate, fresh fish caught from the thawing ponds and rivers, the new soup was started in a clean pot.

Meat—salted, dried, or fresh—could not be eaten during the holy days of repentance and self-examination. Available vegetables were added daily and, after Easter, meat was thrown into the mixture. The fire below was kept burning throughout the year; the kettle provided constant nourishment for the family. Even when vegetables or roots or meat bones were in scant supply, water was added to make a weak broth.

The kettle was a challenge. After eleven months of cooking and several weeks of inattention due to the sickness, Catharina found it caked with thick unrecognizable inedible charred residue. It took her a good hour to scrape out the burnt mess and find the iron insides of the pot. Then, from a remaining snowdrift behind the hut, she scooped up the cleanest snow she could find, put it in the two cooking pots and the hanging kettle and soon had merrily boiling water for her efforts. Reaching far down in the vegetable barrel, she found a large cabbage, some onions, and a few turnips. These, thrown into the pot together with some salt from her own bundle and the last piece of dried fish hanging from the ceiling, filled the small rooms with a delicious aroma.

Meanwhile, Magdalena had bustled about the cottage like a whirlwind. Her first action was to withdraw a tall small-mouthed bottle of vinegar from her bag. Each of the nuns from Grimma had a similar receptacle of the cleansing liquid. She poured some into two small bowls and asked the father to place his coins in one of them. He did so without question. Then, Catharina tore four small squares of cloth which her aunt had dipped in the second bowl. "Keep this in your mouth," she said firmly to the couple as she gave one to each. "It will protect you from danger. And now, please, dear people, please go and lie down in the back room while I ready things here." Their weary eyes reflected their gratitude, and they fell upon the bed.

Back in the main room while the stew was bubbling in the pot, the nuns put the remaining two vinegar-soaked cloths in their own mouths. The next task was to strip both of the other beds of their bedding. Catharina shook out and beat the thin mattresses made of marsh hay sewn into canvas, while Magdalena carried the rest out to the street and set it all afire. She hoped to obliterate the vermin that surely penetrated every thread of the thin quilts. Catharina returned inside the house and with a broom of willow twigs, she destroyed every spider nest within reach.

She opened a jug of ale and set it to warm by the fire. The brew came from the convent storehouse, and Catharina had carried it with her since their departure. Water was tainted and a major source of the sickness, warned the town elders; beer was safe and often served to young and old alike when the water supply was suspect.

VI.

Although it was only early afternoon, the two women had been awake and laboring for more than eight hours. They stopped their work for a short time, sat down, drank, and ate some thick slices of black bread and some steaming bowls of cabbage soup. After resoaking their protective cloths in vinegar, the nuns replaced them in their mouths. Catharina grimaced; the taste was horrible. "You have no choice, sister," chided Sister Magdalena as she opened up more of her own bundles and pulled out clean bedding that she'd brought from the convent; included were some coarse but clean linen sheets and two small blankets. The subject of vinegar was forgotten. She shook her head. "This will never be enough warmth for the woman and her newborn babe," she said softly to Catharina. "We must go to Herr Hochstetter's closets for more."

Without a word, Catharina put on her cape and was on her way back to the big house. She walked quickly, avoiding muddy ruts, a few squealing pigs being chased by their owner, and more twitching rats than she wanted to count. She returned within the hour accompanied by Sister Ave, the two of them carrying some warm quilts, a few baby garments and a small blanket from the lawyer's chest, and a bag of flour. Ave went back to her duties; Magdalena and Catharina began preparations for the birth of the peasant child.

VII.

"Little mother," Magdalena whispered as she awakened the sleeping woman and helped her walk out near the warmth of the fire. As Catharina held up a long towel before the woman, Magdalena removed her stained wrinkled clothing and even though her cap was adorned with the only bit of lace in the house, a tiny strip, she threw it all out to burn in the street. Then the nun gently washed the woman's body and poured warm water and vinegar through her hair. The young peasant stood there in complete silence, a beautiful marble sculpture of motherhood. Only her face, aged far beyond her twenty-four years, betrayed the image; the dark blue circles beneath her eyes and deep wrinkles on her forehead would forever mark these terrible weeks of loss. She was too exhausted, too empty, too full of grief, to speak. The water soaked down into the straw. After drying her, Magdalena led the mother to the clean bed to lie between the clean linens. She placed her own rosary in the roughly calloused hand, put blankets on her, and added her own cloak for extra warmth. The woman curled up on her side and retreated into fitful sleep.

The husband slept on in the back room. Time and again he awoke suddenly and momentarily; the dying moments of his son and the scraping sound of shovels that very morning kept returning to him, tossing him from the unconscious to the awful reality that all his children lay dead and buried beneath the stone cold earth. He wept and fell into a troubled sleep.

Catharina's heart ached for the husband and wife, for the bitter reality of their lives, for their grievous separation from their children. "I thought my life was lonely and empty of light," she cried within her soul. "I never knew. I never knew." Heavy with fatigue and honest sorrow, she sat down at the oak table.

Long shadows began to steal across the village. Early in the evening, the woman abruptly awakened. The first birth pangs surged from her back and steadily increased as they reached around her abdomen like a vise. She said nothing and simply held her breath until the pain subsided. Looking around the darkening room, she saw the two nuns asleep, sitting up with their heads and arms on the table. The baby within her kicked her hands as she cradled her belly. Tears of expectation and apprehension and exhaustion, tears of joy to feel the strong life of a child again, tears of infinite sorrow for her lost children, tears from somewhere and everywhere streamed down her face. The pain rose anew and enveloped her being. But she made no sound.

Catharina woke, instantly alert. She listened intently. Her hands were cold. The howling winds had stopped, but the crisp outdoor air had found its way into the room. Up on the roof, she heard the scampering feet of the rats as they tunneled through the thatch. The fire, burned down to red embers and an occasional flickering flame, sent a faint light about the room. Shivering and disgusted with herself for falling asleep and not tending to the fire, she moved in haste to the woodpile and lifted a large birch log up and into the stove. The dry white bark caught fire immediately and, within moments, orange and yellow beams danced on the walls. There was something comforting about the sounds, the hissing and spitting of the wood; it was a thick log and would burn well for several hours. Everyone else in the cottage seemed to be asleep; Magdalena breathed noisily and deeply as she leaned across the table; the woman did not stir, and no sounds came from the back room. Catharina sat down by the flames and warmed her hands.

The next pain tore through the woman's body with relentless speed. A long moan passed her lips. Catharina jumped up and ran to her side as Magdalena, one ear towards the woman's bed even in sleep, awakened immediately. She felt the hard stomach muscles of the peasant woman straining and tightening; nine months of preparation were over.

Although Sister Magdalena was known for her midwifery skills, Catharina had never before been present at the birth of a child. "Do exactly as I say," the elder nun said firmly to her. Quick to learn but usually too quick to speak, Catharina saw the seriousness of the situation in the eyes of her aunt; she knew this was the time to be still, listen, act, learn, and, if there was time, pray.

VIII.

For a brief span of time after birth, a few priceless moments at most, all humans are equal. Newborns enter the world with innocence and promise. They are clean and fresh and wonderfully made; it matters not if the floor of the birth room shines with highly polished inlaid woods or covers rough boards with scattered straw. These babes mirror the essence of true beauty and purity. Helpless except for a cry and tiny clenched fists to herald their own arrival and claim their place on earth, they depend upon and rightfully expect the wisdom and caring and love of the rest of their race. But that dream disappears quickly. The moments of equality are over. Some are wrapped in the smoothest cotton; others aren't wrapped at all. Some are dearly loved; others are abandoned. Some are greeted with hope and joy while priceless others face a far too short life. Their caretakers, in the form of the communities into which the little ones have been born, often have forgotten the joys of simple things of life. Pomp and pretentiousness, greed thinly veiled in righteousness, overpowering poverty of the soul, the mind, the larder, and not the least, superstition-controlled existence—all these bring shadows into the birthing room. Unwelcome and friendless reality can immediately snatch the child and write a lifelong story of struggle for survival. So it was for the babies born that fateful Saxon spring of 1517. For only a few moments—at most —they were equal with kings.

A quick birth ensued, a blessing for the mother because she was completely spent from the day, the week, the winter. She possessed no reservoir of strength; she would never have survived a long languishing delivery. She barely made a sound throughout the labor, instinctively knowing that every ounce of energy she possessed must be directed positively towards the birth of her baby.

Sister Magdalena knew what she was doing. She had guided many a babe into the world and was well aware of the leading German physician Eucharius Rosslin's words concerning it: "Childbirth is an ordeal for mother and child, who undergo much pain and suffer many grave infirmities, injuries, and accidents." Eighteen-year-old Catharina, however, had scant experience in taking responsibility during any crisis. On this night, she learned from the best nurse in Nimbschen Convent. She watched in amazement at the way her aunt confidently guided the woman through the birth, constantly talking to her, advising her, consoling her, encouraging her. "Come now, little mother, you're almost done. You can do it! I'm right here with you. Squeeze the strong hands of Catharina. Our Lord Jesus watches over you. You are not alone, little mother; I will not leave you. Look at the candle; keep looking at it until the pain is over. Yes, yes, you are doing wonderfully. Rest now for a moment. Breathe deeply; close your eyes. Pray, pray to the Blessed Mother for courage." She soothed; she understood. "Here we go again—hold your breath—look at the candle. Yes, mother, your child wants to be born! It is coming! Your dear, dear babe is almost here! Once more. Ah! Here he is! You have a son! You are a good mother. Thanks to God and all

82

the saints! Glory be to the Virgin, the Father, and the Son! He is beautiful!"

The miracle of birth filled Catharina with tears of joy that would forever remain with her. Here was goodness and beautiful innocence! Here was the future! Here was fulfillment beyond all she had ever dreamed of. As Magdalena attended the woman, Catharina deftly and gently washed the wailing child in warm water mixed with rose attar and a fresh egg and wrapped him in the cloths that she had warmed before the fire. She placed him in the waiting arms of his mother. For the first time in weeks, the mother smiled through tears of loss and joy, first at her tiny son, and then to God in heaven, and, finally, to the two nuns. "Catharina," whispered the older nun, "she has known the death of a son and the birth of a son all in one day. You see a woman that all the world should praise. Surely, she is a saint."

But, of course, in the passage of time, nobody remembered this peasant woman. Neither one book nor scrap of paper nor verse of poetry would mention her name; no portrait artist would ever paint her likeness; she wouldn't learn to write her own name and, certainly not, her memoirs. She symbolized a never-ending stream of hard-working poor people who for centuries forged the human chain in the march of culture and civilization by their forgotten toil and determination to live. Where is the finely sculpted statue commemorating this woman? Who hears music written in her honor? She was as willing to give her life for her children as any decorated general who bravely leads his soldiers into battle. She provided instinctive and wholehearted strength in time of crisis more often than any prime minister or prince. She felt deep concern for the eternal life of her sons and daughters as seriously as any priest. It would not be an exaggeration to say that this woman was greater than they; yet, she had no servants, not one legion, no assembly, nor any college of cardinals for guidance and support. This young mother stood alone. Without a trace, she disappeared into the misty nights and unremembered days of history. Nobody knows her name.

IX.

As was the custom, the priest was called immediately to baptize the child. Only too often, the newborn did not live long enough to wait even a few days for the sacrament. Sisters Catharina and Magdalena stayed with the peasant family of three for another week. Then they moved on to other tasks and missions of aid in the town. The pestilence slowly ran its course. Clean, fresh April air warmed Jüterbog. The most careful citizens continued to worry and drink vinegar and chew several cloves of raw garlic a day to ward off any lingering demons of disease. For the rest, the winter of unspeakable sadness loosened its hold and ordinary life began again.

On the day before the Nimbschen nuns were to return to Grimma, the town buzzed in excited expectation. The old priest, who no longer had death on his face, announced, "Praise God! A glorious day is coming! The end to our grief beckons! There remains hope for our fallen townsmen and for us. The honored emissary of the Holy Church of Rome, Father Johann Tetzel, walks among us tomorrow. Gather up your coins! Ready yourselves! It will be a day to cast off sin and suffering!"

The local priest had no inkling that he was actually heralding the historical event that forever changed Christendom—the Protestant Reformation.

CHAPTER EIGHT

"*Therefore we conclude that a man
is justified by faith, without the deeds of the law.*"

—Romans 3:28

"So halten wir nun dafur, daſſ der Menſch gerecht werde ohne deſ Geſetzeſ Werke, allein durch den Glauben."

—Lutherbibel, Romer 3:28

1517

I.

In the sixteenth century, the Church was virtually a kingdom unto itself. It levied taxes, required tithes, bought and sold titles, operated vast properties, and operated as a lucrative financial institution. Despite challenges from kings to scholars, it controlled the minds, hearts, and purses of Western Christendom.

Old stubborn and cantankerous but beloved Pope Julius II, the benefactor of Michelangelo, died in 1513 amidst sorrowful and prolonged mourning. His successor was thirty-seven-year-old Leo X. This son of two powerful Medici and Orsini families who had been named a cardinal at sixteen, this short man of ample girth and excessive appetite, literally almost disappeared under the weight of the triple tiara and the papal robes. Figuratively, however, he enjoyed to the utmost his position as pontiff. He nodded, blessed, and waved his pearl-encrusted and perfumed gloves to the adoring populace that lined the streets of Rome as he passed by. The position offered the magnificence of endless banquets serving delicacies such as peacocks' tongues cooked in cloves and nuts, entertainment including masked balls and theatrical comedies, together with the trappings of power to which the Medicis were accustomed.

Pope Leo X inherited more than a rich treasury and a powerful papal throne. His heritage included a partially built St. Peter's Basilica in Rome that was meant to rise as the most magnificent religious and architectural structure in all of Europe. The massive church had already cost huge sums of money; the Holy See was in debt to nearly every banking house in Rome and paid interest up to 40%. The great building was far from complete, and Leo determined that he would find a way to finish the elegant shrine built over the tomb of St. Peter and avoid the disgrace of historians writing that he had presided over its decay. He looked to Germany for financial support.

The German Church was the richest of all the papal territories. The parish priests, however, were not partners in this wealth; many of them were forced to have other jobs to meet their simple costs of living, and most of them had little more material goods and security than their peasant parishioners. This was not true, however, of the worldly and pretentious officers of the Church, the bishops and archbishops. The religious priest who was the most Christ-like in theology or action did not win these envied positions; it was no secret that the ecclesiastical offices from cardinal to archbishop were bought by the highest bidder. Rewards were great. Lavish possessions and powerful influence over the princes of Germany were part of the bargain and remuneration. Money was not spent on the poor; it was taken from them. These chancery dues, tribute from kings, consecration fees, and papal taxes poured into Rome to add to the magnificence.

This fleecing of the central European Christians did not go unnoticed. "The Germans have been treated as if they were rich and stupid barbarians, and drained of their money by a thousand cunning devices," declared the Chancellor of the Archbishop of Mainz as far back as 1457. "For many years Germany has lain in the dust, bemoaning her poverty and sad fate. But now her nobles have awakened as from sleep; now they have resolved to shake off the yoke, and to win back their ancient freedom."

The hopeful prophecy took some time to materialize. Some sixty years later, Rome was still milking thousands from Germany. Pope Leo X, determined to fulfill his mission to complete St. Peter's, now had a most fortunate connection—Albrecht of the family of Hohenzollern, the recently appointed and highly cooperative new Archbishop of Mainz. To raise the fee for his own confirmation over and above several other wealthy men who desired the post of archbishop, Albrecht borrowed heavily from the Fugger Banking House of Augsburg, the richest in all of Europe, which had a large part in most papal negotiations in the country. The head of the Fugger financial empire was the son of a merchant and the grandson of a weaver. He had amassed his riches with ownership of farmlands, factories, banks, and mines. He was the rare private citizen who later dared to tell the emperor what to do and when to do it. The pope wanted twelve thousand ducats, in honor of the twelve apostles, as the price for the archbishopric. Albrecht counter-offered with seven thousand—to commemorate the seven deadly sins. The two finally settled on ten thousand. Albrecht won the office, but he was heavily in debt to the Fuggers.

Fortunately, this agreement was more than an appointment.

It was also a most advantageous situation for Pope Leo and his purpose to clear the weeds from around the half-built St. Peter's. His plan provided a solution for the debts of Albrecht, the payment of the princely sum to the Fuggers, the completion of St. Peter's, and his own reputation —all in a surprisingly simple package. First, the archbishop, together with the pope, announced the renewal of Pope Julius II's indulgence. Secondly, half of its proceeds remained with Albrecht to repay the Fuggers; the other half belonged to Pope Leo and his building project.

St. Peter's Indulgence was not limited to Germany. Many emissaries of Rome were dispatched to other countries to sell the papers of forgiveness. Rulers objected to the monies being sent from their own realms. Remembering that the Holy See was a political as well as a spiritual power, it had the power to overcome such problems with made-to-order solutions. For example, Francis I of France was allowed to retain a certain percentage of the sales; Henry VIII of England kept one-fourth of the money. King Charles I of Spain, who was to become Emperor Charles V, was given special treatment. In Saxony, however, the agreement was to send half to Rome and retain the other half to pay off the Fuggers.

II.

I absolve thee first from all ecclesiastical censures, in whatever manner they may have been incurred, and from all thy sins, transgressions, and excesses, how enormous so ever they may be, even from such as are reserved for the cognizance of the Holy See.

—plenary indulgence announced by Pope Leo X
and offered by Johann Tetzel

Indulgences were a product of the Crusades. In simple terms, they were rewards for doing some special act. Initially, they were given to those who risked their lives warring against the unbelieving Turks. In addition, in early days, a man could also win satisfaction by making pilgrimages to holy places or by practicing self-denial, such as promising to live on only bread and water for months or years. They were later offered to people who contributed and substituted money for acts of penance to keep the Crusaders in the field. The practice was such a lucrative moneymaker that the indulgences were extended to cover all sorts of building projects in the Church.

> May our Lord Jesus Christ have mercy on thee, and absolve thee by the merits of His most holy Passion ... and I, by His authority, that of his blessed Apostles Peter and Paul, and of the most holy Pope, granted and committed to me in these parts, do absolve thee.
>
> —the plenary indulgence

As the years passed, the indulgences continued to further develop as a means of justification for sin in the eyes of the Church and, incidentally, in the eyes of God. The Sacrament of Penance had consisted of confession of sin, absolution from the priest, and satisfaction, including imposed acts of alms, fasts, prayers, or self-denial. In 1393, Pope Boniface IX had a new and marvelous idea: he officially made the rewards of inestimable value. They replaced the penance and became immediate certificates for forgiveness of sin, any sin. He signed and sealed thousands of letters of remission that were given to whichever man or woman who had enough silver to purchase one. The indulgence included confession, penitence, and satisfaction. This proof and promise of forgiveness meant that the owner could not ever be punished for his sin; it also subtracted eons from one's stay in purgatory, that vague and terrible resting place of all the dead while they awaited the embrace of heaven.

And as the keys of the Holy Church extend, I remit to you
all punishment which you deserve in purgatory on their
account.

—the plenary indulgence

How could this incredible good fortune be believed? The
Church had a logical answer. It taught that the saints had done
far more good than necessary to achieve their own eternal life;
their extra good works were kept in a treasury by the Church,
which was now more than willing to generously disperse them
among the sinful and thus reduce personal punishment, if the
sinner chose to pay the price.

I restore you to the holy sacraments of the Church.

—the plenary indulgence

In 1476, the rules changed somewhat. Pope Sixtus IV
increased the desirability of purchasing indulgences with the
stunning proclamation that they could also be bought for those
souls already departed! Anyone could erase his own guilt, need
to confess, and horrendous stay in purgatory together with that
of long-dead friends and relatives—with just a simple clink of the
coin.

I restore you to that innocence and purity which you possessed at baptism.

—the plenary indulgence

Pope Julius II had instituted the St. Peter's indulgence in his
original plan for the construction of the basilica. It was this
reward that Pope Leo chose to offer again to the masses. St. Peter's
would rise and its glory would be unsurpassed!

III.

The most notable of all the indulgence merchants commissioned by Rome was a Dominican friar, Johann Tetzel, who was now about to bring his wares to Jüterbog in the year 1517. He represented not only the pope, but the Hohenzollerns. Highly skillful in the art of persuasion, he was endorsed and hired by Archbishop Albrecht who was in partnership with the pope to manage the presentations and sales of the indulgences. Tetzel had been credibly selling indulgences for more than fifteen years, despite the fact that his personal history included a threat of being thrown in the river in a sack as punishment for adulterous behavior.

On one documented occasion, a Leipzig nobleman had asked Tetzel if indulgences could be purchased for a future sin; the answer was affirmative, if immediate payment was received. On the way out of the city, Tetzel was given a severe beating by the nobleman who said that this was the "future sin" he had already been forgiven! Duke George, patron and prince of Leipzig, who usually had no compassion or kindness for anyone, saw some humor in the incident and let the matter die.

For personal remuneration, Tetzel received 80 florins plus all travel expenses for himself and his entourage which included three horses. Now, accompanied by a Fugger banker who kept track of the money and valuables, he swept into town with well-rehearsed and successful drama. A procession of priests, monastics, councilmen, and pious parishioners met him with great celebration. Welcoming banners flapped in the breeze, local musicians played drums and bells, and candles were lit in every window. Following a splendid red cross adorned with the papal arms which was said to be equal with the cross of Christ, Tetzel marched into Jüterbog past the gabled town hall and to the market square carrying the proclamation of indulgence, the papal bull. Signed by the pope with direct authority from Almighty God, the bull was placed upon a gilded cloth high above the cheering crowd of sinners, which included the group of nuns from Nimbschen Convent.

> When you die the gates of punishment shall be shut, and the gates of paradise of delight shall be opened, and if you shall not die at present, this grace shall remain in full force when you are at the point of death.
>
> —the plenary indulgence

Tetzel would much rather have spent his energy in the prosperous university town of Wittenberg, a few miles down the road. But Wittenberg was in north Saxony, and its prince, Frederick the Wise, had no time for either Tetzel or the newly announced indulgence. Neither did he have any intention of permitting more Saxon monies to filter through Tetzel's sly fingers on their way to Rome. Frederick had a checkered past as far as cooperation with the pope; furthermore, he had his own indulgences to sell. He had made Wittenberg a vast storehouse of relics—a thorn from the crucifixion crown of Christ that was certified to have His blood upon it, teeth and hair from various saints of the Church, a straw from the stable in Bethlehem, a strand of Jesus' beard, one of the nails that pierced his hand, three pieces of Our Lady's coat, a piece of bread from the Last Supper, and a twig of Moses' burning bush, just to name a few. Over nineteen thousand sacred relics composed the collection, which was offered for viewing to those buying indulgences. The reward guaranteed by these indulgences was the reduction in purgatory of up to 1,902,202 years and 270 days. This formidable offer of indulgence was not enough to keep curious Wittenbergers home, however. When they heard that the famous preacher Tetzel was in Jüterbog, they traveled the short distance to become part of the sacred magic show. Martin Luther, the pastor and professor in Wittenberg, sent a plea to Albrecht and other bishops to end the raging preaching of Tetzel, but he had no success. In fact, Johann Tetzel then accused Luther of heresy and summarily built a pile of dry wood upon which "all those should be burned who spoke against my indulgences."

Only hours away from beginning their return trip to Grimma, the nuns joined the jostling noisy crowd of country folk, eager to hear, to pay, to be rid of sin and pain and purgatory. Under the papal cross, Tetzel preached that whoever buys a pardon receives not only forgiveness of his personal sins, but would also escape punishment in life on earth and in purgatory.

"God and St. Peter call you! Yes, you!" The monk of the moment swept his arm in a broad circle over the heads of the people; he called them to attention with his loud demanding and cajoling voice. The crowd hushed immediately.

> Listen now, God and St. Peter call you. Consider the salvation of your souls and those of your loved ones departed. Don't you hear the voices of your dead wailing parents and others who say, 'Have mercy upon me because we are in severe punishment and pain. From this you could redeem us with small alms and yet you do not want to do so. Why are you so cruel and harsh that you do not want to save us, though it only takes a little?'

A few children chasing a squawking chicken were scooped up and quickly silenced by their peasant parents. It seemed that the wind did not dare to blow. Friar Johann Tetzel himself was in town.

> You, priest; you, nobleman; you, merchant; you, virgin; you, matron; you, youth; you, old man; enter now into your Church, which is the Church of St. Peter and visit the most holy Cross. It has been placed there for you, and it always cries and calls for you. Are you perhaps ashamed to visit

the Cross with a candle and yet are not ashamed to visit a tavern? Are you ashamed to go to the apostolic confessors, but not ashamed to go to a dance? Run for the salvation of your souls. Be as careful and concerned for the salvation of your souls as you are for your temporal goods!

Catharina and the other sisters from Nimbschen stood close to each other near the front of the gathering. She stared in curiosity and wonderment at the flesh and blood emissary of His Holiness, the archbishop, and God. Standing tall, he spoke in a powerful and commanding tone, full of knowledge and authority, to all of them—to her!

"Visit the most holy cross erected before you and ever imploring you."

"Hear me, you sullen sinners, one and all!" he roared to the assembled citizens of Jüterbog and those who had traveled several miles on foot or by ox cart. He wore the garb of a friar, in contrast to the finely embroidered apparel of his aides who stood behind him. He was not a particularly commanding figure; his face was dominated by a strong jutting chin, flabby cheeks, an aquiline nose, and heavy eyebrows. Catharina could not see his eyes; they were closed as he raised his head and then his arms to the skies in a whispered unintelligible prayer. Following his example, she closed her eyes. The silence was long, and every moment or so she quickly stole a glance at him to see what he was doing. The scene upon the stage was unchanged.

"What are you thinking about? Why do you hesitate to convert yourself? Why don't you have fears about your sins? Why don't you confess now to the vicars of our Most Holy Pope?"

He began to speak softly and smoothly. "My dear people, I bring you greetings and words from Rome. Pope Leo has sent me, a lowly monk, in his stead. Listen, listen to me." He paused, looking over and slightly smiling at the crowd. "The Death and the devil and horrible disease have dwelt in your homes, on your streets, and within your unclean bodies and black hearts." The people nodded in solemn agreement. His pace quickened; his voice was stronger. Every word was clear and calculated.

"Why do you still live? Why are you here to eat and drink and dance? Can you tell me why you survive when your fathers and your children lie cold in the grave? Have you any purpose of worth, of significance, upon this earth?"

Catharina now saw his piercing eyes looking directly through her and she shuddered, vividly remembering each foul day and night of weeping and treacherous sickness and death that she had witnessed for so many weeks. His words were undoubtedly true—after all, he was speaking for the pope—why should one such as she be spared?

"Have you considered that you are lashed in a furious tempest amid the temptations and dangers of the world, and that you do not know whether you can reach the haven, not of your mortal body, but of your immortal soul?"

Speaking in ever-louder tones, Tetzel continued. "Yes, the answer is a resounding 'Yes!' You live and breathe and are here today because you, dear folks, have been chosen to rip away years and eons of punishment in purgatory for those who died this terrible winter! Listen to the voices of your dear dead relatives and friends, weeping and beseeching you and crying, 'Pity us, pity us. We are in dire torment from which you can redeem us for a penance.'" He paused again, his eyes searching the faces for tears trailing down weathered cheeks. Finding several, he patted his ample belly and closed his thin lips tightly. Suddenly, he screamed in professed agony. "Do you not wish to redeem your own? Open your ears! Hear the father saying to his son, the mother to her daughter, 'We bore you, nourished you, brought you up, left you our fortunes and land, and you are so cruel and hard that now you are not willing to set us free for so little. Will you let us lie here in fear of flames? Will you delay our promised glory?!'"

There was no actor in all the traveling troupes wandering Germany that springtime who could hold a candle to the dramatic performance of flair and persuasion of Johann Tetzel. With well-tested expertise, he controlled his audience from the oldest stone-faced farmer to the youngest patrician son.

"Consider that all who are contrite and have confessed and made contribution will receive complete remission of all their sins."

Oh, the indulgence of St. Peter's was a grand bargain by anybody's standards. In a generous gesture, the Pope allowed payment according to one's means. Royalty and the high nobility could buy salvation for twenty-five gold florins. The well-heeled bishops and archbishops of the Church were charged the same fee. Other lesser members of the nobility and cathedral clergy paid twenty apiece to erase their sins. Lower nobility, lawyers, and simple parish priests and prelates got by for six. One piece of gold or twenty coins of silver was expected from the common citizens who composed most of those congregated in Jüterbog. For nine ducats, a pardon could be bought for sacrilege and perjury. Witchcraft and adultery were worth two. Benevolent mercy was offered. Papal concern for the salvation of all permitted even the sick and destitute to be granted an indulgence in exchange for a minimum of fasting and prayers, given according to the judgment of the preacher-vendor of the day. Monastics with no family of monetary merit such as Sister Catharina and her fellow nuns were in this category if they could offer nothing. Everybody was graciously and generously included in this sixteenth-century holy carnival!

"Oh, those of you with vows, you usurers, robbers, murderers, and criminals, now is the time to hear the voice of God. No sin is too evil to benefit from this papal indulgence."

Catharina was quite caught up in the religious fervor. She did not notice that, next to her, Sister Magdalena was decidedly unmoved by the rhetoric; in fact, the elder nun was completely unimpressed with the antics being played upon the stage and muttered something under her breath. Catharina leaned eagerly towards her aunt; "Perhaps we should offer some sort of payment or good works to purchase one of his indulgences. I was thinking of my mother…"

Magdalena turned to her with steely eyes. "Your sainted mother? Enough, Catharina. I do not wish to hear another word from you. It's time for us to leave. Come now and …"

"But, Aunt, he has only started," she interrupted impatiently. "Did you hear what he said? The indulgence can lead my mother out of purgatory! Please, Aunt!"

This was too much. "Do not speak of your dear mother at this performance of nonsense and dishonesty," answered the woman in a loud disgusted whisper, loud enough for Tetzel to notice that he did not hold everyone present in fixed adoring attention. He glared at the group of nuns; Magdalena stared right back, gathered up her charges, and whisked them away from the gathering. Tetzel's voice followed them as they departed. "Will you not, for even a quarter of a florin, receive these letters of indulgence through which you are able to lead a divine and immortal soul into the fatherland of paradise?"

IV.

As soon as the money rattles in the box the soul jumps free
of hellfire's knocks.

—Johann Tetzel

"Sobald daſ Gold im Kaſten Klingt die Seele auf dem Fegefewar
ſpringt."

—Johann Tetzel

The nuns of Grimma left Jüterbog for their own convent with
no indulgences in their pockets and no peace in their hearts, for
they had seen and heard one of their respected own openly show
disgust towards an emissary of the Church. The code of strict
obedience had been broken in public.

Tetzel did admirably well for the Church that day in Jüterbog. Convinced that the man was closely akin to an angel of
God, most of the citizens could barely believe their good fortune
in being offered such a magnificent blessing, despite their obvious undeserving nature. They bought the indulgences as fast
as they could empty their money pouches. After doing so, as a
convenience, a minter in the papal entourage accepted jewelry,
flattened it, and stamped out shiny new coins to purchase more
parchments for flight from purgatory. And the Fugger bankers
counted the bounty as promised, half for themselves in payment
of the Archbishop's debt, half for the rising dome of St. Peter's in
Rome. The hard-earned coins would buy neither bread nor shoes
for the Jüterbog peasants in April of 1517; rather, the silver opened
the heavy doors of the dreadful halls of penance and easily
closed the pages of guilt for sinner after sinner. What miracles
the Church offered that lovely spring day!

In the name of the Father, and of the Son, and of the Holy
Ghost. Amen

—the plenary indulgence

98

V.

As so often happens as the pages of civilization turn, unnamed folk are the vital link between events that grab the headlines and become momentous history. On this occasion, the catalysts proved to be a few simple suspicious Wittenbergers who witnessed and succumbed to the salesmanship of Tetzel and then decided to find out if their newly bought indulgences were as good as promised. There was something about the whole affair that bothered them. On the short trek home, a day's walk, they decided to get the opinion of their trusted parish priest, Dr. Martin Luther. Their questions and fears were unrecorded, unwritten, but forever remembered.

The cleric, the instructor of philosophy and religion, the man of burning passion where the Scriptures were concerned, reacted with anger and disgust at the charade played upon the people from his city, his university, his congregation. It was on this day that he decided to once again challenge Rome itself in a scholarly but determined way. It was not the first time. In fact, the year before in 1516, he had preached against indulgences, asserting that nobody could know whether or not contrition was honest and deserving of the remission of sins. He had come to the monumental conclusion in his study of the book of Romans that salvation was based upon the mercy and grace of God, upon simple faith, not condemnation. Grace and forgiveness could not be bought like a book or a new hat or a sack of onions. With other scholars, he had discussed his theory, which he felt was supported by St. Augustine who had written eleven centuries before that the saved "are singled out not by their own merits, but by the grace of the Mediator; they are justified . . . as by a free favor."

Many years later in 1541, Luther recounted the event:

> It came to pass in the year 1517 that a preacher monk called Johannes Tetzel, a noisy troublemaker whom Duke Heinrich had already sent packing in Innsbruck . . . the same

Tetzel is now peddling the indulgences and divine grace for money, as dearly or cheaply as he can. At that time I was a preacher in the monastery here and a young doctor, newly left home, passionate and enthusiastic about the Holy Scriptures. When many Wittenberg folk ran after indulgences to Jüterbog, and as truly as the Lord Jesus Christ has redeemed me, I knew not what this indulgence might be, as indeed no one knew. I began to preach outright that one could do something better, and more certain, than buying an indulgence.

Now, in 1517, with smoldering dissatisfaction, he sat down to write his objections to the blatant misuse of his beloved church and his Master, Jesus Christ. As a monk who espoused poverty, he first assailed the grandiose construction of St. Peter's in Rome declaring, "The revenues of all Christendom are being sucked into this insatiable basilica. We Germans cannot attend St. Peter's. Why doesn't the pope build it out of his own money? He is richer than Croesus. He would do better to sell St. Peter's and give the money to the poor folk who are being fleeced by the hawkers of indulgences."

Secondly, wearing the academic and argumentative hats of a university professor, he challenged the papal claim to have access to the keys of purgatory; forgiveness of penalties comes from God and the sacrament of penance, not from the words of one who has no access to leftover good deeds. Luther wrote:

The saints have no extra credits. If there were any superfluous credits, they could not be stored up for subsequent use. The Holy Spirit would have used them fully long ago. Therefore, I claim that the pope has no jurisdiction over purgatory. If he does have the power to release anyone from purgatory, why in the name of love does he not abolish purgatory by letting everyone out? If for the sake of miserable money he released uncounted souls, why should he not for the sake of most holy love empty the place?

Finally, as priest to the souls in his congregation, Martin Luther directly attacked the whole theology of indulgences, and, at the same time, those seated in high-church places who created and approved them. Here, he approached being guilty of heresy:

> Indulgences are positively harmful to the recipient because they impede salvation by diverting charity and inducing a false sense of security. Christians should be taught that he who gives to the poor is better than he who receives a pardon. He who spends his money for indulgences instead of relieving want receives not the indulgence of the pope, but the indignation of God. Peace comes in the word of Christ through faith. He who does not have this is lost even though he be absolved a million times by the pope.

Martin Luther intended to provoke a public debate among theologians and scholars on the validity of indulgences in the same manner that arguments were often addressed in the university town of Wittenberg. His action at that point was not to cause a rebellion against the Church, but to discuss the nature of indulgences and why they were not biblical, canonical, or justifiable.

Some months after Tetzel's circus in Jüterbog, on October 31 of 1517 and according to the custom of the day, Luther's arguments known as the Ninety-Five Theses were pounded upon the north door of Castle Church in Wittenberg. They were prefaced by the following written announcement:

> Out of love and concern for the truth, and with the object of eliciting it, the following heads will be the subject of a public discussion at Wittenberg under the presidency of the reverend father, Martin Luther, Augustinian, Master of Arts and Sacred Theology, and duly appointed Lecturer on these subjects in that place. He requests that whoever cannot be present personally to debate the matter orally will do so

in absence in writing. In the name of our Lord Jesus Christ.
Amen.

Some of the points set down for academic and theological discussion are as follows:

1. When our Lord and Master, Jesus Christ, said "Repent," He called for the entire life of believers to be one of repentance.

8. The penitential canons apply only to men who are still alive, and, according to the canons themselves, none applies to the dead.

10. It is a wrongful act, due to ignorance, when priests retain the canonical penalties on the dead in purgatory.

11. When canonical penalties were changed and made to apply to purgatory, surely it would seem that tares were sown while the bishops were asleep.

24. It must therefore be the case that the major part of the people are deceived by that indiscriminate and high-sounding promise of relief from penalty.

27. There is no divine authority for preaching that the soul flies out of the purgatory immediately when the money clinks in the bottom of the chest.

28. It is certainly possible that when the money clinks in the bottom of the chest avarice and greed increase; but when the church offers intercession, all depends in the will of God.

32. All those who believe themselves certain of their own salvation by means of letters of indulgences, will be eternally damned, together with their teachers.

36. Every Christian who truly repents of his sin has complete remission of all pain and guilt, and it is his without any letters of pardon.

37. Any true Christian whatsoever, living or dead, participates in all the benefits of Christ and the Church; and this participation is granted to him by God without letters of indulgence.

43. Christians should be taught that one who gives to the poor, or lends to the needy, does a better action than if he purchases indulgences.

45. Christians should be taught that he who sees a needy person, but passes him by although he gives money for indulgences, gains no benefit from the Pope's pardon, but only incurs the wrath of God.

50. Christians should be taught that, if the pope knew the exactions of the indulgence-preachers, he would rather the church of St. Peter were reduced to ashes than be built with the skin, flesh, and bones of the sheep.

55. The pope cannot help taking the view that if indulgences (very small matters) are celebrated by one bell, one pageant, or one ceremony, the gospel (a very great matter) should be preached to the accompaniment of a hundred bells, a hundred processions, a hundred ceremonies.

62. The true treasure of the church is the Holy gospel of the glory and the grace of God.

67. The indulgences, which the merchants extol as the greatest of favors, are seen to be, in fact, a favorite means for money-getting.

68. Nevertheless, they are not to be compared with the grace of God and the compassion shown in the Cross.

79. It is blasphemy to say that the insignia of the cross with the papal arms area is of equal value to the cross on which Christ died.

81. This unbridled preaching of indulgences makes it difficult for learned men to guard the respect due to the pope against false accusations, or at least from the criticisms of the laity.

86. Again: since the pope's income today is larger than that of the wealthiest of wealthy men, why does he not build this one church of St. Peter with his own money, rather than with the money of indigent believers?

92. Away, then with those prophets who say to Christ's people, "Peace, peace," where there is no peace.

95. And let them thus be more confident of entering heaven through many tribulations rather than through a false assurance of peace.

—from Martin Luther's Ninety-Five Theses

VI.

Martin Luther expected a debate. He got a reformation.

Unknown to him, not too many miles away in Nimbschen Convent, there lived a young nun named Catharina von Bora whose strength, intelligence, vitality, curiosity, and patience throughout the journey of her life would play a tremendous part in his own march of faith.

Chapter Nine

I commit my soul to the mercy of God through our Lord and Saviour Jesus Christ, and I exhort my dear children humbly to try to guide themselves by the teaching of the New Testament in its broad spirit, and to put no faith in any man's narrow construction of its letter here or there. In Witness whereof I the said Charles Dickens, the testator, have to this my last Will and Testament set my hand this 12th day of May in the year of our Lord, 1860.

1483–1519

I.

Negative reaction to the posting of the 95 Theses and its explosive aftermath was not particularly theological, academic, sympathetic, nor philosophical, to say the least!

Within three weeks I shall have the heretic thrown into the fire.

—Johann Tetzel

Brother Martin has a fine head, and the whole dispute is nothing else than an envious quarrel of monks. [And soon thereafter ...] A drunken German has written these theses; when he sobers up he will think differently of the matter. [And later ...] Luther is a child of ruin, a grim enemy of our salvation.

–Pope Leo X

A simple friar who goes counter to all Christianity for 1,000 years must be wrong ... Therefore, I am resolved to stake my lands, my friends, my body, my life and my soul to defend the Church of Rome.

–Emperor Charles V

I do not wish to dispute with that beast anymore, for he has deep eyes and strange ideas in his head.

–Cardinal Cajetan

Poor monk, thou hast truth on thy side, brother Martin, but thou wilt not succeed. Get thee to thy cell and pray, "O God, have mercy upon me."

–Dr. Albert Kranz of Hamburg

An indignant Tetzel reacted swiftly. In November, he journeyed to the University of Frankfort where he gained the support of an eloquent professor, Conrad Wimpina. Together they refuted Luther with what became known as Tetzel's "One-Hundred and Six Anti-Theses" in defense of the doctrine of indulgences. He presented them to an assembly of three hundred monks in January of 1518. Following are some of his positions:

3. Christians should be taught, that the Pope alone has the right to decide in questions of Christian doctrine; –that he alone, and no other, has power to explain, according to his

judgment, the sense of Holy Scriptures, and to approve or condemn the words and works of others.

4. Christians should be taught, that the judgment of the Pope, in things pertaining to Christian doctrines, and necessary to the salvation of mankind, can in no case err.

8. Christians should be taught, that they who conspire against the honour or dignity of the Pope incur the guilt of treason, and deserve to be accursed.

17. Christians should be taught, that there are many things which the Church regards as certain articles of the Catholic faith, although they are not found in the inspired Scriptures or in the early Fathers.

44. Christians should be taught to regard as obstinate heretics all who, by speech, action, or writing, declare that they would not retract their heretical propositions, though excommunication after excommunication should be showered upon them like hail.

50. Christians should be taught, that they who scribble so many books and tracts … who side with those who preach or write such things … must expect to plunge themselves and others along with them, into eternal condemnation at the great day, and the deepest disgrace in this present world. For every beast that toucheth the mountain shall be stoned.

Eight hundred copies of Tetzel's document were sent to Wittenberg where they were burned by the students. Others expressed support and encouragement for Luther.

Aha! He'll do it! He is come for whom we have waited so long! The time has come when the darkness in churches and schools will be dispelled.

–Dr. Fleck of Wittenberg

My dear Brother Martin, if you can storm and annihilate purgatory and popish huckstering, then you are indeed a great man.

–an old Low-German clergyman

Take care of the monk Luther, for a time may come when we may have need of him. Truly his propositions are not to be despised; he will show wonders to the monks.

–Emperor Maximilian in a letter to Elector Frederick the Wise

Truly the yoke of Christ would be sweet, and His burdens light, if petty human institutions added nothing to what He Himself imposed. He commanded us nothing save love for one another.

–Erasmus of Rotterdam, Catholic humanist and intellectual

Erasmus, whose wisdom was sought after by clerics, kings, and academicians, chose to remain with the Church. He felt that education of the masses was the key to the necessary reform and the rise of independent thinking, but he knew that such change would be very long in coming. A twentieth century Catholic historian, John F. Acton, concluded, "Erasmus belonged, intellectually, to a later more scientific and rational age. The work which he had initiated, and which was interrupted by the Reformation troubles, was resumed at a more acceptable time by the scholarship of the seventeenth century."

Others were not willing to wait for that gradual reform. Among those who exhibited tremendous courage with increasingly precarious actions and writings were John Hus, Jerome of Prague, John von Wesel, and Johann Wessel Gansfort.

Jon Hus (1369-1415), was a Bohemian professor and dean of the faculty of arts at the university in Prague and beloved priest of the Bethlehem Chapel in that city. He was popular with the people because he preached in Czech and taught them how to sing hymns together as part of their services. He was held in high esteem by the nobility and was chaplain to Queen Sophia. Along with his radical worship changes, Hus preached reform of papal power and debated against the practice of indulgences, the infallibility of the pope, and the existence of purgatory. He declared that the Church should possess no worldly possessions and that the final spiritual authority was scripture and individual interpretation, not the pope. He wrote, "To rebel against an erring pope is to obey Christ." After excommunication by both the Archbishop and Rome, arrest, imprisonment, and condemnation followed when he affirmed his beliefs and refused to recant. The fiery pyre of dry kindling and branches was prepared, and he was burned at the stake. Within the rising smoke and flames, Jon Hus was heard singing until he could sing no more.

The Holy Roman Church continued to punish heretics with death by fire. As early as 1307, Pope Clement V had made a Frenchman, Bernard Gui, a tool of the Inquisition. Gui faithfully recorded his sentences with great efficiency; his "Book of Sentences" survives to this day in the British Library of London. In addition to the sentences of 633 persons in fifteen years, the book includes chillingly matter-of-fact itemized accounts of expenses including the following costs for a Sunday execution of four people who deserved torture by fire, according to the judgment of the church authorities:

For large wood—55 sols, 6 deniers
For vine-branches—21 sols, 3 deniers
For straw—2 sols, 6 deniers
For four stakes—10 sols, 9 deniers
For ropes—4 sols, 7 deniers

For the executioner, each—20-80 sols
In all—8 livres, 14 sols, 7 deniers

To show the mercy of the Church, the accused was given a last chance to recant. If he did not, the lighting of the fires was handed over to secular executioners. As Pilate had washed his hands of the death sentence handed down to Jesus as recorded in the Book of Matthew, the religious judge fourteen centuries later followed suit, avoiding personal action, and could say, "See ye to it."

To put things in sad perspective in the annals of history and humankind, 385 long years later in 1692, the Protestant authorities in Salem, Massachusetts, likewise declared the execution of common folk for their own superstitious and theocratic purposes. They, too, in their ignorance, were obsessed with witches and the veiled methods of Satan.

The chief supporter of Hus, Jerome of Prague, was soon branded a heretic against Rome and was executed by fire ten months after Hus in May of 1416 in the same public square. As recorded by witnesses, his words to the executioner were, "Come in front, and light it before my face; if I had feared death I should never have come here." The onlookers heard fragments of agony and melody until he choked. A hundred years later as Martin Luther was studying church history, he came upon the writings of Hus. He struggled with the actions of the Church against one "who could write so powerfully. I shut the book and turned away with a wounded heart."

In 1466, John von Wesel, a professor at the university in Erfurt, dared to teach that prayers to the dead and indulgences were false dogma His words, "I despise the pope, the Church, and the councils, and I worship only Christ" made him a certain target of the Inquisition. He was condemned but later recanted to spend the rest of his days in prison.

Almost unknown in later centuries, a man by the name of Johann Wessel Gansfort (1420?-1489) preached that faith was the only path to salvation and that all the practices of the Church from confession to absolution to purgatory were false. Some decades later in 1522, Luther came upon his words and wrote that "if I had read his works before, my enemies might have thought that I had borrowed everything from Wessel, so great is the agreement between our spirits."

More than 300 years later, the respected Catholic historian Johannes Janssen summed up the situation in the not-so-Holy Roman Empire and its political and spiritual ally in the Vatican:

> The contrast of pious love and worldly greed, of godly renunciation and godless self-seeking, made itself apparent in the ranks of the clergy as well as in other classes of society . . . The higher ecclesiastical orders . . . enjoyed abundant and superfluous wealth, which many of them had no scruples in parading in such an offensive manner as to provoke the indignation of the people, the jealousy of the upper classes, and the scorn of all serious minds.

II.

In the middle of the night of November 10, 1483, St. Martin's Eve, a second son was born to Hans and Margarethe Ziegler Ludher in a stone house in the Saxon town of Eisleben, Germany. Because of high infant mortality, newborn babies were baptized quickly. This little child was baptized the next morning at 11 am in the Late Gothic church of Saints Peter and Paul on St. Martin's Day. He was named for the saint of the day, St. Martin of Tours, the patron of drinking and merriment. Art and carvings in the church honored St. Anne, the mother of the Virgin Mary and patron saint of miners.

The peasant parents had moved with their first son to Eisleben, a mining town, from their ancestral village of Moehra.

Hans, a hot-tempered man born in 1459, was the eldest son in his family. There were four brothers—Big Hans, Little Hans (the black sheep of the family with many arrests and convictions), Veit who married a woman from another farm which gave him a home, and Heinz who was named for Grandfather Heine. They were free peasants and their surname was Luder, or Lytter, or Ludher, or Luther; spelling and pronunciation varied with the hamlet and level of society. The German language was spoken by all, but rarely taught or written. In that century in the rural areas, ultimogeniture, not primogeniture, was the accepted manner of inheritance; the youngest son, not the oldest, remained on the family property. As a result, Big Hans had left to work in the copper mines of Eisleben. When the new baby was six or seven months old, they moved again to a nearby town, Mansfeld. Martin recalled, "My parents, at first, were very poor. My father was a poor miner, and my mother often carried the wood upon her back in order to raise us children. They endured many hardships for our sake." There would be nine children in the family; some died in infancy, which was only too common. As in any century, each loss of a newborn is heart-wrenching; in the 1500's, it was sadly expected. Within six years, the hard-working father bought shares in two small smelting works and would one day become part owner of six mines and two furnaces and serve on the town council.

Theology of the times was full of sin and fear. Parental discipline was harsh, and whippings were common punishment. "My father once chastised me so severely that I fled from him and avoided him until he won me to himself again." Nevertheless, the father recognized intelligence in the boy, and at the age of seven, he was sent to school where he studied reading, writing, singing, and Latin, and he served the church as an altar boy. Discipline in the school was even more strict than at home, and religious instruction served to terrify the pupils. "From youth I was trained to turn pale at the very mention of Christ's name, for I was taught to regard Him as a severe and angry judge."

Lucas Cranach the Elder of Wittenberg was a skilled portrait painter and a close friend of Luther. He was known as a talented realist; his subjects were painted as they appeared complete with wrinkles and blemishes. His paintings revealed an uncanny depiction of the personality of the individual. In 1527, he painted the aging Hans and Margarethe. Hans, with untamed hair and a set-in-stone jaw, seems rather disgusted with time spent posing and completely unafraid of confrontation or challenge.

The mother, her head tightly covered with a simple long white scarf, is portrayed as a stern time-worn woman who had seen years and years of hard work and weariness. She stares into space with eyes that had seen too much trial, cried too many tears, saw and accepted long lonely hours (see image gallery, I-3).

Like most peasant folk, the mother Margarethe feared the unknown evils that surely dwelt in the deep, dense, and dark fir forests. She taught her children to be wary of witches and elves who could appear in any form from a toad to a deer. From childhood on, her little ones were made aware that thunder and lightning storms, with their fierce piercing winds and heavy downpours, came as punishment from above for wrongdoing. Forgetting prayers could bring the wild weather and anger from God and the saints; the gentle breeze was a result of good behavior. Her children were told that evil spirits lurking in the shadows could make the crops fail and curse the cows and goats so that they would give soured milk. Many illnesses were believed to be unnatural and caused by enchantment of the servants of the Devil. A priest might force a witch to disappear, but he could lose his own life in the process. Death, an obsession with the Day of Judgment, and the vast unknown were everywhere present. It is little wonder that these ingrained beliefs passed on from one generation to another—from grandmother to mother to child—combined with the certain penalties sure to come from a frightening omnipotent God who watched from the heavens. Fear of this stern God controlled and permeated the days and long dark nights of childhood and persisted into young adulthood and old age.

Martin's father sent him to Magdeburg, a large commercial center and a member of the Hanseatic League, for further education in a school run by the Brothers of Communal Life. Because of his poverty, the boy and many other students were compelled to beg and sing for food at the doorsteps of the citizens. Within a short time, however, he followed the wishes of his parents and enrolled in St. George's School in Eisenach, a much smaller town of three to four thousand people where his mother had relatives. Martin seemed to have mixed feelings, calling it both "my beloved city of Eisenach" and a "god-forsaken place full of clerics." It was true that one in ten inhabitants was a clergyman, and it did have three churches and seven monasteries. Lessons were usually taught and learned by constant repetition in chorus by the class. He sang in the Church of St. George where Johann Sebastian Bach would be christened and sing as a youth almost two hundred years later in 1685. As in the last town, he was forced to repeat prayers in public and sing for crumbs of food until he was noticed by the well-to-do wife of a merchant, Frau Ursula von Cotta, who took him in, fed him, and cared for him as a mother would do. One bit of advice Frau von Cotta gave to seventeen-year-old Martin was this: "There is nothing so fine as the love of a good woman—if you can find her."

At a farm called Zulsdorf, not too far away, a baby girl named Catharina was born to the Hans von Bora family.

III.

In 1501, Martin's first studies were completed. His father, who had by this time become a rather successful foundry owner, had the fervent hope that his scholarly son would then study law and become a distinguished jurist, a man of high standing who could give comfort and honor and grandchildren to his aging parents. The university at Erfurt, a beautiful large city with 36 monasteries and 90 churches and more than fifteen thousand citizens, was chosen, and Hans supported his son as much as possible "by his bitter sweat and toil." As recorded, the name of the new student was one among many: "Martinus Ludher ex Mansfeld." Beginning each day with prayer and attending mass, it was at this school that the young man studied the "seven free arts": grammar, rhetoric, Aristotelian dialectics, metaphysics, geometry, music, and astronomy in preparation for a legal course of study. Graduating second in a class of seventeen, he became proficient in Latin and brilliantly earned both his Bachelor and Master of Arts degrees by the age of 21 on January 7, 1505. During those years, the young scholar began giving lectures in the arts and practiced the skills of argument. This was also the first time he was permitted to page through a Holy Bible. The priceless book, printed in Latin, was chained so that no wandering, unlearned, or disrespectful hands could touch or steal it.

The study of law was not to be. A life-threatening accident when he nearly bled to death, the horrors of the Black Death taking the lives of three close friends, and the continual desperate concern and conviction that he was a most unworthy sinner plunged him into melancholy. Then something of powerful consequence happened that was to change his life forever. In early July of 1505 while traveling alone near Erfurt, he was caught in a terrifying and dangerous thunder and lightning storm. Facing death and the certain punishment of God that was so strongly embedded in his mind from his youth, he cried for help and vowed to St. Anne, his father's patron saint, to become a monk if he would survive. **"Ich will ein Münch werden."** It was not an idle promise.

Despite his father's rage and disappointment, Martinus quickly entered the austere community of the Hermits of St. Augustine Monastery in Erfurt. Hans Luther was suspicious of the whole event, hoping that it was not orchestrated by the Devil in the guise of holiness. The fearful quandary was constantly present in the peasant world; the word was 𝕬nfed)tung, which means a trial might be sent by God to give strength, or it could be a clever plan of the Devil to consume your soul. Which interpretation was true this time? His father was pacified only because he had just lost two younger sons to the plague and was urged by clerics "to offer something to God."

This was the same summer when six-year-old Catharina von Bora of Lippendorf was enrolled in school in Brehna and then soon returned to her family farm, because her father could not meet the cost of her tuition. This was also the year that her father remarried.

Martinus, the young monk, dedicated his hours and days and nights in his search to find tranquility with God. He embraced unquestioned obedience with far more diligence than was required in the strict order. He served as doorkeeper, swept the church, and cleaned the latrines. He fasted three days at a time, welcoming the weakness of body, but righteousness was not to be found. Hoping to imitate the physical sufferings of Christ, he slept in the cold without a cover. Lengthy prayers upon his knees on the rough stone flagstones gave no lasting communion with his God. Critical and constant self-examination to achieve humility only served to feed the sin of pride. If repentance was incomplete, then absolution and forgiveness was lost. Poverty of possessions proved to be poverty of spirit. He could never do enough. His vicar, the kindly Staupitz, tried to console him as a kind spiritual father would. But Luther was inconsolable. "I was a good monk, and I kept the rule of my order so strictly that I may say that if ever a monk got to heaven by his monkery it was I. All my brothers in the monastery who knew me will bear me out."

Just one year later, Martin Luther was ordained in the Erfurt

Cathedral. His father had accepted his son's path and donated twenty gulden to the priory kitchen. On May 2 of 1507, the fledgling priest read his first Mass and later said, "When I celebrated my first Mass in Erfurt and read the words, 'I sacrifice to You, the living, only God,' I was so terrorstricken that I felt like running away from the altar ... For I thought: who is it you are speaking to? ... Who am I, that I should lift up mine eyes or raise my hands to the divine Majesty? ... For I am dust and ashes and full of sin and I am speaking to the living, eternal, and the true God."

Scholarly study continued. He was sent to the Augustinian monastery in Wittenberg in 1508 where he taught moral philosophy as well as logic and ethics while studying theology. That same year, Catharina von Bora entered Nimbschen Convent of Grimma as a nine-year-old.

In 1509, the young Luther returned to Erfurt to lecture and teach a general studies course. Then a mission to settle a monastic dispute ordered by his monastery and Staupitz fulfilled a long-held dream, a pilgrimage to the Holy City, to Rome.

Monks were to walk, not ride, so the chilling forty-day journey of about 800 miles over the Alps that late fall of 1510 was made on foot. This was the only time that he was to step beyond the borders of his native country. St. Peter's Cathedral, which was to play a primary part in Luther's later thoughts and actions, had not been built, but at its site the foundation stone had been dedicated. The monk was shocked to discover that the city was not the shining City of God he had imagined nor the place for the religious renewal and redemption that he so fervently desired. He found that many of the priests coarsely boasted and laughed with irreverence about the sacraments; some quickly read the Mass so that they could be paid for performing another one. Greed masked as holiness becomes the sure child of pride that without notice can destroy the purest of intentions, philosophies, religions, and, most seriously, souls.

He saw urban and moral decay everywhere. Thieves

infested the center city and cows roamed the hut-lined streets in contrast to the ornate lodgings of the clerics. He and hundreds of other pilgrims paid a fee to view the ancient bones of 46,000 martyrs. Money alone was hardly the root of all evil in Rome. He hoped to gain merit for his grandfather in purgatory by climbing Pilate's stairs on his knees, leaving a prayer and a kiss on each step. Nevertheless, what he saw and heard filled the young priest with doubt.

Had the Church largely abandoned the message of its Founder with spiritual superficiality? Disillusioned, he left the busy squalid city and returned to the quiet of the Augustinian Monastery and the university's academic atmosphere in the rather provincial and sleepy town of Wittenberg.

IV.

After two years of further study, on October 18 and 19 of 1512, he was awarded a doctoral degree in theology at Castle Church and prepared to continue to teach at the University of Wittenberg. Unable to pay the fees for the degree, he was granted the cost by the Elector Frederick the Wise with the promise that he would lecture at the school for life and also serve as preacher, speaking twice each week at St. Mary's Church, the most ancient building in the city. Obviously, the Elector did not intend to let the esteemed scholar slip away from his territory.

When a serious academic scholar focuses and fastens upon a new idea, theory, or revelation, his curiosity and determination to research further cannot easily be squelched. When that passion is further accompanied by an inner emotional turmoil and life exeprience that directly applies, the search for truth becomes even more intense; there is no turning back. When that thirst for knowledge plus the personal hunger for answers is influenced and enveloped by one's religious beliefs, the door to answers and enlightenment cannot be closed, even in the face of persecution.

So it was for the young professor and preacher, Martin Luther. For many hours of every day he read the ancient classical writers and studied the Holy Bible, his source material. Still, in spite of his searching, he had not been able to find peace nor comfort nor affirmation from God. Despite hours of study, fasting, confessing, scourging, and acts of penance and humility, he felt worthless. He recognized that all he read and preached and taught and said was answerable to the long history of Christianity. This meant that Martin Luther could not stop searching. His journey and quest for truth were just beginning.

Despite hours and months of study and doing good works, young Luther could find no peace for his soul. He simply was not good enough to face God. Neither physical nor psychological self-deprivation gave relief to the hollow-cheeked monk. Soul-searching was fruitless; confession of sins known and unknown did not matter. He was in torment because he could not remember all his sins and was driven to the abyss of despair and wrenching guilt. Dreadful superstitions that marked his childhood and society around him, as well as the fearsome promise of certain condemnation for disobedience to the Church, defeated him at every turn. He could not save himself. Pride in humility was unforgivable. He could not satisfy God.

The monk's inner agony combined with his academic intelligence did not go unnoticed by Staupitz. For Martin, this man was mentor, vicar, confessor, and surrogate father who had the wisdom and vision to be all four. Believing that the young man could best heal his anguish by serving and healing others, Staupitz intervened and resigned his own academic seat at the University of Wittenberg, leaving it open for the best possible candidate—Martin Luther, who was already known to be a thorough theologian, vigorous preacher, and brilliant professor. He was chosen for the position with the approval of Elector

Frederick who, incidentally, rarely spent time in Wittenberg, preferring to be an anonymous benefactor.

Wittenberg, known for citizens given to excessive drinking and reveling, was described by one sixteenth-century observer as "a poor, insignificant town with little, old, ugly wooden houses." This small town was an unlikely place for a young professor to shake the foundations of the most powerful religious institution of the western world. But shake it he did. His platform was a medieval university classroom and students, a professor's desk and books, and a young preacher's pulpit. Luther would himself go on to author and publish upwards of 50,000 pages open to study and rebuttal. From his teachings, common people would draw a new sense of personal dignity and respect.

V.

Martin Luther's study of Scripture related to deserving and obtaining salvation had been brewing for some years. He pored through the available writings of the earliest Christians. From 1513 through 1516, Luther had studied the Latin, Greek, and Hebrew translations of Scripture, given lectures, and urged discussion on the Psalms, Romans, Galatians, and Hebrews. The distressed cry of Psalm 22, "My God, my God, why hast thou forsaken me? Why art thou so far from helping me?" which was echoed in the words of Jesus as he hung dying on the cross, mirrored the desolation that the monk had felt in the depths of his being for so many years. But why should the Son of God feel so deserted? As he studied the New Testament, he began to find an answer. Because Jesus was true man, he felt the agony of isolation and the huge burden of pain that came from carrying the guilt of all. As Luther read on and on, he perceived the simple concept of justification and relief by faith. Half in terror and half in joy of what he had found, he encountered and accepted the words of Romans 1:17 ("The just shall live by faith") and Galatians 2:16 ("Knowing that a man is not justified by the works of the law, but by the faith of Jesus Christ"). These were words that could not be disputed by prince or pope. Liberation from guilt was a gift! It could not be bought because it was not for sale. His years of fasting, pilgrimages, floggings, poverty, and enforced humility to raise himself in the eyes of the Almighty had been empty acts. As he came out of the depths, he dared to preach and teach that good works would surely follow faith; not the other way around. True benevolent charitable actions done to better the lives of others must spring from looking outward to the needy rather than inward to save oneself from dishonor in the eyes of God. He said, "These passages in Paul opened for me the gates of paradise. I felt I was born again."

As he lectured in his classroom and preached with passion from his pulpit at the town church of St. Mary, he slowly but surely moved away from and challenged current teachings of the Church. Men and women must be able to bravely and confidently face God without the intercession of a priest or saint. His friends and fellow friars began to show great concern for him. There certainly were other reformers in the Church, but they simply could not or would not stand up and declare their beliefs. When Luther was asked to preach in Duke George's city of Dresden, he did so espousing the merits of grace rather than indulgences and all the sacraments. The duke said that such preaching "would only make the people presumptuous and mutinous." Perhaps it did. Nevertheless, Luther continued to speak.

The time was ripe. Events were coming together. With mounting resentment, the German electors and the citizens were attempting to separate themselves from the control of Rome. The printing presses were oiled and ready to roll. Student unrest and daring vitality were buoyed up by the distribution of essays railing against authority, printed broadsheets and engravings with political overtones, and satirical cartoons that were printed by the hundreds. A venue for communication for personal thought and a level platform for dissent or acceptance was now available. Literacy mattered. Luther called the printing press "God's last and greatest gift." A new theology was emerging that began to give hope for an end to the vacuum of spirit and soul so prevalent among the unlettered peasants.

As pastor and monk, Martin Luther visited and preached in the outlying districts of Wittenberg. In 1516, he visited the Augustinian monastery of Grimma. Many of its monks were relatives of the nuns in the nearby convent. Some were brothers. On the rare occasions of communication between the two groups, it is only logical to assume that news of the unrest and theological debate in the rest of Saxony was passed from brother to sister. The name of Luther became synonymous with a new and dangerous way of thinking, with a new era of the value of the human mind and soul—for the poor farmer who had barely any personal property to the prince who possessed inherited wealth and position.

The oak tree is a symbol of strength, stubbornness, and individuality. Nobody tells it how to form. It twists and turns and reaches out on its own irregular path to face the sun. Some acorns fall from a healthy branch amid the sunshine and then lie buried in the shadows of the soil; they never germinate. Others will obey a natural instinct to grow, to reach upward towards the sun again. This miracle of God's creation rises up in its own way, not directed nor governed by the demands of others. And so the story of some lives as they struggle and grow and dare to be different has changed the path of history.

Martin Luther was not the only person who was stepping into an unknown future and making life-changing decisions. During the same period of time, young Catharina von Bora took her vows as a nun at Nimbschen Convent of Grimma.

VI.

The year 1517 was the turning point in the struggles and survival of Christianity. That was the year when the famous but fraudulent Johann Tetzel took the sale of his indulgences to Jüterbog, far too close to Frederick's Saxony and to Wittenberg's parishioners. That was the year that Martin Luther decided he had no choice but to publicly and academically address the falsities of indulgences. That was the year on October 31 that he pounded his complaints, his 95 Theses, on Castle Church door, which served as the bulletin board for the university. That was the year that he requested debate in an effort to reform the Church from within. The October winds in Saxony are crisp, cold, and strong as they sigh and sing and boisterously blow through the treetops in the forests and narrow cobbled streets and then into the cracks of churches, shelters, and barns. They will change suddenly without warning. That autumn, perhaps they were the harbingers of what was to come. Events quickly ensued.

Some of Luther's Augustinian brothers begged him to step back, while others urged him to stay the course. He had no intention of retreating into silence. To make sure that he was understood, he wrote a simplified version of the Theses in German. It was printed and spread like wildfire throughout the countryside in just fourteen days and created immediate clamor. Without Gutenberg's printing press, such discussion amongst people other than the highly educated would have been impossible, even unthinkable. Sensing trouble ahead, Archbishop Albert and Tetzel himself urged Rome to condemn Luther. Pope Leo, however, was not too interested and called the situation a monkish squabble.

In the meantime, Luther wrote pamphlets, treatises, and sermons that shifted from indulgences to the misuse of power by the pope, though he felt the holy father had been misguided by his advisors. He also argued that the Roman Church was no higher than the Greek Christian Church. Furthermore, he contended that the sacrament of penance had been falsely required. While studying the scriptures, he discovered that the Latin Vulgate version of Scripture had been mistranslated from the ancient Greek and that "do penance" actually should have been translated "be penitent." Pope Leo and the Roman Curia began to take notice. Getting little support from the Augustinians, Pope Leo commissioned a Dominican cleric to pen a reply to Luther, which declared that he who does not accept the infallibility of the pope or the practice of indulgences as taught by Rome is to be branded a heretic. At this point, the Pope was still not ready to condemn the monk. Other ecclesiastical academics including the eminent Johann Eck, the Vice-Chancellor of the University of Ingolstadt, were ready to storm against him. The young monk was summoned to appear in Rome within sixty days.

Once again, Frederick the Wise stepped in. The pope had written to him:

> Beloved son, the apostolic benediction be upon you. We recall that the chief ornament of your most noble family has been devotion to the Holy See. Now we hear that a son of iniquity, Brother Martin Luther of the Augustinian eremites, hurling himself upon the Church of God, has your support ... We call upon you to see that Luther is placed in the hands and under the jurisdiction of this Holy See lest future generations reproach you with having fostered the rise of a most pernicious heresy against the Church of God.,

Nevertheless, the Elector convinced the Pope that his university professor should not be judged by Italians, but on German soil. Summarily, Luther was ordered to Augsburg in the fall of 1518 to be examined for heresy by Cardinal Cajetan, a prominent Dominican theologian. Concerned that Luther's life was in danger, Frederick arranged for imperial safe-conduct from Emperor Maximillian himself. The sessions in Augsburg with the cardinal ended in impasse. An angry Cajetan refused to allow debate and demanded that the monk recant his errors or face banishment and excommunication. Luther refused and requested permission to allow debate on the points of contention at the universities, but his request was not granted. It was at this time that he no longer gave obeisance to the pontificate, declaring that it was a man-made position and thereby had become the source of the decline of the Church. Cajetan declared that the Pope was the interpreter of Scripture and above all else in the Church. Luther replied, "I deny that he is above Scripture." Cajetan ended the encounter with, "Go, and let me not see you again, unless you recant!"

Luther remained in Augsburg for a week, and then he and his friends, fearing an arrest, passed quietly through the guarded gates of the city by night and fled on horseback to Wittenberg. Luther wrote down his understanding of the events in Augsburg with letters to religious and political leaders. To Duke George, the usually unsympathetic leader of Southern Saxony, he wrote that "a common reformation should be undertaken," possibly the first time the word that was one day to describe the whole historical movement was used.

Cajetan requested Frederick to send Luther to Rome, but the Elector refused. In December of 1518, Frederick the Wise sent a document to the Curia in Rome. In part, it stated:

> We are sure that you acted paternally toward Luther, but we understand that he was not shown sufficient cause to revoke. There are learned men in the universities who hold that his teaching has not been shown to be unjust, unchristian, or heretical. The few who think so are jealous of his attainments ... As for sending him to Rome or banishing him, that we will do only after he has been convicted of heresy ... We will not lightly permit ourselves to be drawn into error nor to be made disobedient to the Holy See. We wish you to know that the University of Wittenberg has recently written on his behalf.

VII.

The year 1519 burst with successive events. The Pope was facing a political crisis and wished for the monk to be quieted, because Emperor Maximilian died in January, and his heir-apparent was young Charles of Spain, of whom Leo did not approve. He preferred the German Frederick or any German from his own backyard and, under the circumstances, showed ambivalent conciliatory actions towards him, particularly in the controversy concerning the Elector's obvious protection of his young professor. The Pope offered the Golden Rose, a highly desired symbol of honor from the papacy, to Frederick along with the wish that he move against "that child of Satan, son of perdition, scrofulous sheep, and tare in the vineyard, Martin Luther." This Golden Rose encrusted with precious stones was carefully and securely packed along with some extra incentives, including an increased indulgence value of 100 years from purgatory for every bone amongst Wittenberg's relics, unencumbered acceptance and position for five papal notaries, and ten dispensations of disability for illegitimate birth. Leo expected that the theological problem would and should be solved quickly. Karl von Miltitz, a Saxon nobleman acting as a chamberlain in Rome, was sent to his home electorate to deliver the rose and its accompanying letter and special gifts from the Pope—in spirit, to Frederick; in substance, to the Fuggers for safe-keeping.

> Beloved son, the most holy golden rose was consecrated by us on the fourteenth day of the holy fast. It was anointed with holy oil and sprinkled with fragrant incense with the papal benediction ...This rose is the symbol of the most precious blood of our Saviour ... Therefore, dear son, permit the divine fragrance to enter the innermost heart of Your Excellency, that you may fulfill whatever the aforementioned Karl von Miltitz shall show you.

Miltitz soon discovered times and allegiances were changing dramatically. His orders were far more difficult to fulfill than either he or the Pope anticipated. Frederick was not so easily moved, nor was the German countryside any longer under the thumb of the Pope. As Miltitz traveled on the rough rural roads and into the hamlets and slept in village inns, he realized that three out of four Saxon Germans were in sympathy with Luther and openly hostile towards Rome. The majority of his own friends were of anti-papal sentiment. Frederick felt unready for the imperial crown; Miltitz could not convince him otherwise. He then offered the possibility that the bothersome monk could even become a cardinal if only the theological nonsense would stop. Again, no progress. The Elector could not be bought. Failing in his papal mission, Miltitz stepped backward and separately agreed to a truce with Luther that there would be no more argument from either side. If the two could make peace, the subject could evaporate. But the sparks of fervent opinion throughout Europe had already been struck; a handshake could not put them out.

At the University of Wittenberg, two faculty professors were in firm support of Luther's writings. One was the older and rather fierce Andreas Carlstadt, who had conferred the doctoral degree upon Luther; he was even more vehement and outspoken about the travesties of the Church than the monk. The second, Philip Melanchthon, a quiet but passionate young teacher of Greek, Latin, Hebrew, physics, and philosophy was already known in collegiate circles to have a brilliant mind. Several universities vied for his scholarship. Despite their offer of higher wages, much to their chagrin he chose Wittenberg because it gave him more academic freedom. Melanchthon became Martin Luther's chief confidant, supporter, colleague, and life-long friend. The influence of these two upon the university students was more than significant; it was crucial during the subsequent months. In addition, a third man and poet laureate of Germany, Ulrich von Hutten, had the ear of the people. A champion of nationalism and humanism, of a country experiencing new-found pride in its own cultural roots apart from the heavy hand of Rome, of peasant folk who had been in the dark for too long, he and his poems became a part of the growing support for the professors of Wittenberg.

The Church was not devoid of advocacy and voice. The esteemed Erasmus urged patience as he wrote to Luther: "Old institutions cannot be rooted up in an instant ... keep cool. Do not get angry. Do not hate anybody. Do not be excited over the noise you have made ... I am pleased with your Commentary on the Psalms." On the other hand, chief among Luther's opponents was the aforementioned Dr. Johann Eck of Ingolstadt. Known to be a formidable and volatile adversary who could fluently win any argument with his uncanny memory and ability to easily corner his adversary, he was more than ready to do verbal battle with the misguided reformers. When he challenged the 95 Theses, the vow of silence made by Miltitz and Luther was broken; it was Carlstadt who replied. Eck requested public debate, and in June it was scheduled at the University of Leipzig under the interested eye of Duke George. The city, incidentally, was only 19.6 miles by foot or wagon through the forest from the convent at Grimma.

Carlstadt was joined by Melanchthon, Luther, several Wittenberg professors, and two-hundred armed university students who feared retaliation in hostile territory. But it was Martin Luther that Dr. Eck wanted. He quickly overpowered Carlstadt with clever and superior verbal tactics to finally meet face-to-face with the man he considered a worthy competitor. An onlooker of the event and professor of poetry, Mosellanus, wrote his observations:

> Martin is of middle height, emaciated from care and study, so that I can almost count his bones through his skin. He is in the vigor of manhood and has a clear, penetrating voice ...
> He has Scripture at his fingers' ends ... He is affable and friendly, in no sense dour or arrogant. Everyone chides

him for being a little too insolent in his approaches ... he is somewhat too impertinent and vicious, more than someone who is treading a new path as a theologian ... Carlstadt is smaller than Luther with a complexion of smoked herring. His accent is thick and unpleasing ... He is slower in memory and quicker in anger. Eck is a heavy, square-set fellow with a full German voice ... His eyes and mouth and his whole face remind one more of a butcher than a theologian. He has a phenomenal memory. If he had an equally acute understanding, he would be perfect.

The debate went on for eighteen days. Johann Eck had finally met his match. Both men relied heavily on their own interpretations, long studies of history, and their ringing rhetorical skills. The pace of speech was slow because the words were laboriously written down by scribes. Far too many bored spectators in their cherished seats fell asleep. But it was the written copy that was published immediately and found its way into the hands of the people; Luther's name became familiar to many who had never owned a book.

Eck stormed against the monk and accused him of committing heresy on several counts, including Luther's denial that the Roman Church was above all others in Christendom, including the Greek Orthodox. Eck accused, "I see that you are following the damned and pestiferous errors of John Wyclif, who said, 'It is not necessary for salvation to believe that the Roman Church is above all others.'" Eck challenged Luther's conclusion that the Pope of Rome was not the supreme bishop in the early centuries and pointed out Luther's agreement on many points with Hus who had been condemned for heresy by the Council of Constance one hundred years before. "If you defend them," Eck stated, "then you are heretical, erroneous, blasphemous, presumptuous, seditious, and offensive to pious ears." Finally, Eck challenged Luther's declaration that the Councils of the Church could err.

Luther roared in return that the Greeks or any other Christians were equal to the papists: "The unity of Christendom could be preserved under numerous heads just as the separated nations under different sovereigns dwell in concord." He argued that Greek Christians who had never accepted the supremacy of Rome surely were given the gift of salvation. He boldly declared that historical study proved that the early church leaders and bishops in outlying districts and countries were subject to neither appointment nor loyalty to the Roman bishop and that the Donation of Constantine which stated otherwise was fraudulent. (This conclusion, based on Luther's research in Leipzig University's own library during a break in the action, proved to be correct by Italian Lorenzo Valla and is accepted by church historians.) He said that Hus had been wrongly executed "because no believing Christian can be coerced beyond holy writ. By divine law we are forbidden to believe anything which is not established by divine Scripture." Purgatory and indulgences were argued but with little discussion. But on the subject of the infallibility of the pope and the meaning of penance, Eck retorted, "Are you the only one who knows anything? Except for you, is all the Church in error?" By his own words, the candid and sometimes reckless Augustinian monk had committed heresy beyond redemption.

Luther was labeled the "Saxon Hus," a name that he deemed an honor rather than a shame. His words rang in the great hall of the Pleissenburg Castle: "I will tell you straight what I think. I am a Christian theologian and I am bound to defend the truth with my blood and death. I want to believe freely and be a slave to the authority of no one, whether council, university, or pope. I will confidently confess what appears to me to be true."

Duke George halted the never-ending discourse that could find no compromise, and Eck's words were, "At any rate, no one is hailing me as the Saxon Hus." By the time the two opponents rode out of Leipzig, both had stood their ground. A letter from Prague to Luther stated, "What Hus was once in Bohemia, you, Martin, are in Saxony." Luther replied, "We are all

Hussites without knowing it." Probably due to the well-publicized debate, he became a leader, an urgent spokesman for thousands of people across Europe. His printed essays and tracts gained readers and enthusiasm in France, England, Spain, and with the free-spirited Swiss. Once again, the printing press played an indispensable part in spreading information to city and village and further into the cells and chapels of monasteries and convents. In the meantime, Johann Eck made his way to Rome to report the declared heresies of the monk. He recommended excommunication. Pope Leo was not amused by his misguided monk in Saxony.

CHAPTER TEN

Here I stand. I cannot do otherwise. God help me. Amen.

—Martin Luther, Diet of Worms, April 1521

Hie ftehe ich. Ich fan nicht anderf. Got helffe mir. Amen.

1520–1523

I.

The winter of 1520 with its deep snows and political turmoil provided a few months of personal reflection, courageous decision-making, affirmation both for and against deeply embedded principles, and several bouts of spiritual indigestion. Was the Church in command powerful enough to overshadow and squelch independence of soul? Could it dictate the thoughts and daily lives of the people? Strangely enough—well, maybe not so strangely—human beings seem to have a difficult time learning from the examples and crises of history, century after century. Will those in high office, both religious and civil, ever learn to rule without falling into the temptations of self-serving greed and egotism? Just one hundred years after all the upheaval in Germany in 1520, which resulted in the Protestant Reformation, a group of determined English pilgrims who felt their religious freedoms were denied—by a Protestant monarch and hierarchy this time—somehow stood up and sailed across an unknown ocean with their little children in a small sailing vessel called the Mayflower. The year was 1620, and the place was Plymouth Rock; the long and dreary and deadly winter piled snow upon snowdrift just as it did year after year in northern Germany. Nevertheless, hope survived. The determination and strength of those ordinary people once again trumped entrenched supremacy. The dangerous voyage across the Atlantic was only the first chapter in their story in the New World. Likewise, back in 1520 in Saxony, the unnamed hard-working common man and woman awakened to the possibility of new life.

II.

*bulla\bul-e n. 1. [ML]. The round lead seal attached to a papal bull.

*bull n. {ME bulle, fr. ML bulla fr L 1: a solemn papal letter sealed with a bulla or with red ink imprint.
2. EDICT, DECREE.

—Webster's Ninth New Collegiate Dictionary

Pope Leo was slow to act. Finally, in June, he made his move to get rid of the great thorn in his side, Martin Luther. What he firmly believed to be haunting heretical thought was steadily creeping and encroaching into his and his Church's territory. He prepared and signed the *Exsurge Domine*, the bull of excommunication. It read in part:

> Arise, O Lord, and judge thy cause. A wild boar has invaded
> thy vineyard. Arise, O Peter, and consider the case of the
> Holy Roman Church, the mother of all churches, consecrated
> by thy blood. Arise, O Paul, who by thy teaching and death
> has and dost illumine the Church. Arise, all ye saints, and
> the whole universal Church, whose interpretation of Scripture
> has been assailed. We sincerely express our grief over the
> ancient heresies which have been revived in Germany. We
> are downcast because she was always in the forefront of
> the war on heresy. Our pastoral office can no longer tolerate
> the pestiferous virus of the following forty-one errors. [they
> are written] ... Now therefore we give Martin sixty days in
> which to submit, dating from the time of the publication of
> this bull in his district. Anyone who presumes to infringe our
> excommunication and anathema will stand under the wrath
> of Almighty God and of the apostles Peter and Paul.
> —Dated on the 15th of June, 1520

The bull condemned the pamphlets, books, and sermons of Luther that could be found and ordered them to be burned; it demanded that Luther recant his heretical beliefs or be formally excommunicated and condemned to die as a heretic and an outlaw. Three months passed before the bull reached Saxony. In the meantime, Luther used the months of relative quiet and put more pen to paper.

The media of the day, the pipeline of information, the broadcast of newsworthy events was that utilitarian and oh so timely invention, the printing press! Luther wrote three pamphlets that became known as the Reformation Treatises; they spread throughout the countryside like the roiling waters of a flood. The first, which was written in German, *Sermon on Good Works* and *Letter to the German Nobility*, attacked Rome on three points: (1) that there is no difference between laity and the clerics because by baptism, all Christians are priests; (2) that because he is a priest, he can interpret Scripture on his own two feet; and (3) that Scripture is the ultimate authority, and it does not say that the pope alone can call together a council. He also addressed the vast gulf between the splendor of Rome and the widespread poverty among the people.

> Some have estimated that every year more than 300,000 gulden find their way from Germany to Italy . . . We here come to the heart of the matter . . . How comes it that we Germans must put up with such robbery and such extortion of our property at the hands of the pope? . . . Who can longer endure it or keep silence? . . . Above all, we should drive out from German lands the papal legates with their "powers"— which they sell for large sums of money—to legalize unjust gains, dissolve oaths, vows, and agreements, saying that the pope has authority to do this—though it is sheer knavery.

The second little book called *The Babylonian Captivity of the Church* was written in Latin to theologians and then translated into German. Luther compared the long centuries of suffering of the Jews by the Babylonians to the last thousand years of captivity of the original Christian Church by the Roman papacy. He addressed the seven sacraments of the Church. From his study of the New Testament, Luther concluded that only two sacraments had been instituted by Christ: the Sacrament of Baptism and the Sacrament of the Altar. He denied the Catholic sacramental belief in transubstantiation. Bread and wine could not change in substance, but did contain the presence of

Christ. Penance, ordination, marriage, confirmation, and extreme unction were ceremonies created by man. He did not object to contrition and confession of the penitential, but to absolution by a priest. Ordination as a sacramental rite only widened the distance between laity and the clergy; the latter would then benefit from special powers. As to the sacrament of marriage, he wrote that "marriage between believers and non-Christians should not be banned; . . . a heathen is just as much a man or a woman created by God as St. Peter, St. Paul, or St. Lucy." He was now openly attacking prescribed doctrine of Rome; he was challenging dogma. The man could be eloquent and fiercely stubborn, and sometimes urgency rather than patience ruled.

Luther sent his third essay, *A Treatise on Christian Liberty*, to Pope Leo in November 1520. Many scholars consider it his finest work. He wrote "unless I am deceived, it is the whole of Christian living in a brief form." In it, he expressed his belief that faith alone, not works, makes a Christian. "The tree bears fruit, the fruit does not bear the tree." It declares that the priceless freedom offered to the faithful comes with the responsibilities of serving others, of loving one's neighbor, of being a ministering priest. For him, the resulting humanitarian religion supplied the answer to years and years of commands and sacrifices and the fears based upon the demands of the Holy See.

Together with the essay, a personal conciliatory letter was sent to the pope; "I look upon you less as Leo the Lion than Daniel in the lions' den of Babylon ... I am sending you a tract as an auspice of peace, that you may see the sort of thing with which I could and would more fruitfully occupy myself if your adulators would leave me alone." It is unknown if the pope ever read either document. At any rate, the Holy Father did not respond in kind. The bull had already been published and approved by the Vatican; Luther's books had been publicly burned in the Piazza Navona. The bull was delivered to Luther on October 10 and to the rest of Rome's dominion by two of Pope Leo's honored nuncios, Jerome Aleander, the trusted former rector of the University of

Paris and scholar of Greek, Latin, and Hebrew, and Dr. Johann Eck, the same staunch advocate of Rome in the Leipzig debates.

The Pope was the ultimate power; his words were to be unquestioned. The bull was printed by the Church; its words were irrefutable. The two nuncios, blessed and sent by the Pope, were to distribute the document, to burn all heretical writings, and to be respected as separate emissaries. Aleander was assigned to deliver the bull to the Low Countries, the Rhine, and to the court of the emperor. Eck's travels were to cover all other territories, the universities, and the bishops. Such a mission of righteousness, such a grand and holy endorsement, such an enhancement of self-image, such a step to higher and honorable and important office and repute!

However, the man tilling the rocky soil, the scholar studying in the university, the woman learning to read, and even some monastics emerging from their monasteries stood up and questioned, refuted, and withheld respect. Such a blot upon the reputation of the nuncios. Such public rejection. Such disgrace.

Eck met with unexpected opposition from the bishops, some of whom set aside the bull for six months; the electors feared disorder amongst the populace; the University of Wittenberg declared that "the goat should not be permitted to be a gardener, nor the wolf a shepherd, nor John Eck a papal nuncio." Students, professors, and even clergymen at Erfurt threw copies of the bull in the swirling waters of the Gera River. In Torgau, the papal documents were targets of mudballs, pulled down from public places and torn to pieces. In Leipzig, Eck feared for his life and hid in a monastery, then fled the city where he had been so prominent during the debates. He did find success with the bishops of Meissen, Brandenburg, and Merseburg, and, as a result, declared his relief on a tablet in his old Ingolstadt University church:

John Eck, professor ordinarius of theology and university
chancellor, papal nuncio and apostolic protonotary, having

published in accord with the command of Leo X the bull of Lutheran doctrine in Saxony and Meissen, erects this tablet in gratitude that he has returned home alive.

Aleander did not fare any better. Expecting support from Erasmus, he got these words instead: "The inclemency of this bull ill comports with the moderation of Leo . . . Papal bulls are weighty, but scholars attach more weight to books with good arguments drawn from the testimony of divine Scripture, which does not coerce but instructs." The royal court at Antwerp welcomed him, but students at the book burning also threw in works of Roman theology.

The public executioner of each town was duty-bound to light the fires, but in Cologne, he at first refused to obey; in Mainz, supported by a large noisy crowd, the executioner declined to act. Aleander hired the local gravedigger to do the deed the next day. The fire was witnessed only by a few women and their geese. Citizens threw stones at the esteemed emissary. He informed the pope of the serious uprisings against the Church and repeated his warning that for some time many Germans had been "waiting for 'some fool' to open his mouth against Rome."

In times of turmoil, poets dare to write the words that speak from the hearts of the common man and find their way into the language of the streets. Ulrich von Hutten listened to the resistance and riots in the countryside and dangerously reflected and published the following verse translated by Roland H. Bainton:

O God, Luther's books they burn,
Thy godly truth is slain in turn.
Pardon in advance is sold,
And heaven marketed for gold.
The German people is bled white
And is not asked to be contrite.
To Martin Luther wrong is done—
O God, be thou our champion.

My goods for him I will not spare,
My life, my blood for him I dare.

The printers who published the poem were thrown into prison.

Another poet and engraver, Hans Sachs, did not add to Luther's popularity. Sachs published Luther's comments concerning the clergy, which claimed that their mission was to spread God's word, not to institute rituals by which to make money. He urged craftsmen to change their ways. The craftsmen did not appreciate Luther's views. The livelihoods of goldsmiths, masons, sculptors, bell casters, miniature painters, and carpenters were threatened. After all, they made the objects that were used in the required rituals.

It was on the tenth of December of 1520 at 10 am that the students at Wittenburg responded. They congregated at Elster gate at the invitation of Melanchthon who invited "pious and studious youths" to build their own bonfire. They threw scholastic theology, papal decrees, and the canon law into the flames. Luther himself tossed in the bull. He wrote, "Since they have burned my books, I burn theirs. The canon law was included because it makes the pope a god on earth." Frederick the Wise continued to uphold Saxon law and excuse Luther:

> After I left Cologne, Luther's books were burned and again
> at Mainz. I regret this because Dr. Martin has already
> protested his readiness to do everything consistent with the
> name of Christian, and I have constantly insisted that he
> should not be condemned unheard, nor should his books be
> burned. If now he has given tit for tat, I hope that His Impe-
> rial Majesty will graciously overlook it.

The Reformation had solid roots. Events of consequence were underway.

III.

At the tender age of 21, his Imperial Majesty Charles V carried huge burdens upon his narrow shoulders. An heir of several royal households, by the age of sixteen he was already in control of lands from Holland to Spanish America. With loans from the Fuggers, who appeared to bankroll just about everybody, he had been elected and crowned Holy Roman Emperor. Despite fragile health and mounting responsibilities, the very young emperor did have an expedient sense of diplomacy and wisdom with respect to the German Electors. After a good deal of posturing and discussion among himself, Aleander, and the Curia together with the steady influence of Frederick of Saxony who had one hand in the Vatican and two feet firmly planted in Germany, the decision was made. Charles V declared that a German could not be condemned without trial in Germany; Luther would be tried at the Diet of Worms in April of 1521.

The legendary ecclesiastical city of Worms, known as oldest city in Germany, could not have been a better symbolic stage for the official conclave. It was the site of the ancient myth of Siegfried the Dragon-slayer, the hero of Richard Wagner's primitive and majestic opera on a colossal scale, *The Nibelungen Ring*. This vast musical panorama told the passionate epic of life, a potent story rooted in the thousand-year-old folklore of Worms. As described by Wagner's biographer, Dr. Oliver Huckel, "It is a dream of yesterday and a vision of tomorrow, if we have eyes to look into the heart of the mystery."

The respected old halls, rooms, stone walls, narrow winding streets, and church towers hid many shadows, secrets, and stories. In the sixteenth century, the city was honored and vitally alive and bursting with expectation. Time changes things. Some three hundred years later, a well-known literary visitor from England wrote:

Worms is a fine old place, though greatly shrunken and decayed in respect of its population; with a picturesque old cathedral standing on the brink of the Rhine, and some brave old churches shut up, and so hemmed in and over-grown with vineyards that they look as if they were turn-ing into leaves and grapes.

–Charles Dickens, 1846

The Diet was the formal assembly of the princes and other dignitaries of the German nation called together by Charles V as King of Spain and Emperor of the German lands to address a number of profound problems that he faced. These included trouble with France, invasions by the Turks, and the support or lack thereof from the pope. As the winter winds of January through March whirled about, the trial of the wayward monk was just one of the challenges to resolve. Those attending, the electors, the papal sympathizers, the citizen representatives and nobility, and the clergy, had other ideas. They came to Worms to see Martin Luther live or die. Night or the morning—which was it to be? Which dragon would be slain? The pope or the monk? The nuncio Aleander was quite aware of the forces of discontent:

All Germany is up in arms against Rome … Papal bulls of excommunication are laughed at. Martin is pictured with a halo above his head … I cannot go out in the streets but the Germans put their hands to their swords and gnash their teeth at me. I hope the Pope will give me a plenary indulgence and look after my brothers and sisters if anything happens to me.

March 3, 1521: Aleander proposed the condemnation of Luther to the members of the Diet, which in response requested a hearing. The Emperor promised Luther safe-conduct passage from Wittenberg.

April 2: Luther left Wittenberg. Approaching Worms in a two-wheeled cart, he was met by a protective band of knights and two thousand citizens. Riots by the peasant 𝔅𝔲𝔫𝔡𝔰𝔣𝔥𝔲𝔥 if the Diet condemned Luther were whispered and threatened.

April 17: Luther stood alone before the Diet and its intimidating and awesome court. The finely dressed observers watched but were irrelevant. Even so, they did not yawn and sleep this time as many had at the earlier debate between Luther and Eck. This was the meeting, the confrontation of two men—one, a simple son of a peasant miner in monastic garb; the other in all his regal glory, the ruler of vast territories and heir of generations of Catholic sovereigns, including Ferdinand and Isabella and the long line of Hapsburgs. The eminent chronicler of Luther's life, Roland Bainton, wrote these words about the prophetic event: "Here the past and the future were met. Some would see at this point the beginning of modern times."

The scene was set. A table was covered with a pile of Luther's books and writings. He was asked two questions by an official of the Archbishop of Trier: "Are these words yours?" and "If they are, will you retract all that is written therein?"

The monk replied, "The books are all mine, and I have written more."

The examiner asked, "Do you defend them all, or do you reject a part?"

Luther answered, "This touches God and his Word. This affects the salvation of souls . . . To say too little or too much would be dangerous. I beg you, give me time to think it over."

The emperor granted him one more day.

April 18: In a larger and very crowded chamber at six o'clock in the evening, Luther again appeared before Charles V. After much detailed discussion and debate, Luther finally concluded his argument in German and again in Latin:

Since Your Majesty and your lordships desire a simple reply,
I will answer … Unless I am convicted by Scripture and
plain reason … I cannot and I will not recant anything, for
to go against my conscience is neither right nor safe. God
help me. Amen.

The text above was copied in the earliest handwritten transcript.
The first printed version also included the words: "*Here I stand, I
can not do otherwise.*"

And there he stood.

April 19: The Emperor replied.

.After having heard yesterday the obstinate defense of
Luther, I regret that I have so long delayed in proceeding
against him and his false teaching. I will have no more to
do with him. He may return under his safe conduct, but
without preaching or making any tumult. I will proceed
against him as a notorious heretic.

April 20: Four of the six Electors concurred with Charles.
Ludwig of the Palatinate and Frederick of Saxony dissented. The
𝕭𝖚𝖓𝖉𝖘𝖈𝖍𝖚𝖍 placards went up throughout the city.

April 26: Luther left Worms for Wittenberg and disappeared
along the way.

May 6: The Emperor proclaimed the Edict of Worms to seal
the fate of the monk. It declared his sins against Rome in graphic
detail. It commanded "one and all not to house, shelter, give food
or drink to nor entertain the said Martin Luther, nor to provide
him in word or deed either secretly or openly with any kind of
help, support, succour or encouragement, but wherever you see

him arrive or enter, if you are able, to take him prisoner and send him to us." It declared the following conclusion:

> We have labored with him, but he recognizes only the authority of Scripture, which he interprets in his own sense. We have given him twenty-one days, dating from April 15 ... when the time is up no one is to harbor him. His followers also are to be condemned. His books are to be eradicated from the memory of man.

May 26: Charles V signed the document in the presence of Aleander. By this time, Martin Luther was nowhere to be found and thought to be dead, ambushed by the enemies of the Reformation. The prominent artist from the Netherlands, Albrecht Dürer, feared this was true and wrote in his personal journal, "I know not whether he lives or is murdered, but in any case he has suffered for the Christian truth. If we lose this man, who has written more clearly than any other in centuries, may God grant his spirit to another ... What might he not have written for us in the next ten or twenty years?" All this news found its way into the walls of the many religious orders throughout the countryside; the monastics as well as the peasants began to look at their lives with both a certain fear and the fresh air of freedom of thought.

IV.

May 4: The condemned monk had been ambushed, not by enemies, but by friends in a plan instigated by Frederick the Wise and much to Luther's disapproval, for he wanted to return to Wittenberg to prepare for a certain end. On the pretext of visiting his grandmother and other relatives in Eisenach for possibly the last time, his wagon turned onto an isolated road through the woods in the dark of night. Only he and one of his traveling companions knew of the plan. Suddenly, they were accosted by five men on horseback. Luther was knocked to the ground and thrown upon a horse. Surrounded by his captors, he disappeared into the forest. By Frederick's design, he was taken to the massive ancient Romanesqe castle of Wartburg south of Eisenach. This fortress, where the relics of St. Elizabeth were kept, was complete with a formidable wooden drawbridge, owls and bats, and the Devil lurking in dark corners. Luther was safely hidden at the castle until early 1522. Disguised and dressed as a knight with a heavy beard, he spent the months in a relative solitary existence and was known as Junker Jörg.

For a man so accustomed to strong and often boisterous reaction to his words, to the daily joy of challenging students, to interactive debate with his colleagues on everything from philosophy to Philippians, and to all the sounds of the people in the streets, the sedentary isolation forced upon him was like unto prison. Despite all his talents, he was not a master of silence. His diet was poor, he suffered from insomnia, and he had little exercise. His health, physically and psychologically, suffered greatly. He did demand to write to Melanchthon and a few others, and, miraculously, the secret of his survival was kept. He agreed to remain in seclusion, but only until Easter of the following year. To fill up the long hours and the onset of depression, Luther wrote numerous tracts, sermons, and essays and began the monumental task of translating the entire New Testament into the vernacular German.

Communication. Communicating the Scriptures to the people—this was the purpose of the task of the translation. Luther lived and breathed the importance of this connection. He felt that the Hebrew-to-Greek-to-Latin translators had little interest in the common language of the people and its everyday usage. About this, Luther wrote:

The very letters of a language have their own individual
looks and airs, which have to be respected. If Moses and
the prophets were to rise again, they themselves would not
be able to make sense of what they are supposed to have
said ... I try to write German, not Latin or Greek couched in
German. You don't get your German from the Latin ... you
get it from the mother in the home, the child in the street,
the man in the market place ... Sometimes it takes a fort-
night to find just the right expression for one single word.

Even Duke George gave him some credit! "One thing about that
absconding monk is you can learn the use of German from him
right well." Luther later said, "I don't want to boast—but I think
you will find it better and more useful than all the Greek and
Latin versions and commentaries put together, for the stumps
and stones are cleared out of the way so that everyone will be
able to read it without stumbling-blocks ... This version won't
last forever ... In time the world will need something new again."

Without the presence of a strong leader, passion without
vision was heating up in Saxony. Intended reform now created
both chaos and relief. Chaos, because some new oppressors guided
by self-righteousness rather than righteousness arose, and relief,
because the murmurs of a few now gave strength and purpose
to a chorus of many. Meanwhile, monastic life began to crumble.
Thirteen monks left the Augustinian cloister in Wittenberg.

Luther found sufficient reason to leave the sheltered walls
of Wartburg for Wittenberg twice. The first was for only a few
days, arriving on the fourth of December 1521. To his dismay,
a destructive anti-papal riot had erupted in the once peaceful
academic town. The day before, impatient students and some
revolutionary-minded citizens swarmed into churches and the
Franciscan monastery, threw stones, destroyed lamps and books,
and intimidated priests. Luther, still disguised as a knight but
recognized by many, quickly warned against such thoughtless
behavior. "Violence will only make the Antichrist strong. Preach,

pray, but do not fight." Not everyone listened. A friend in Wittenberg later recalled the visit. "When I saw Martin in 1522, he was somewhat stout, but upright, bending backwards rather than stooping; with a face upturned to heaven, with deep, dark eyes and eyebrows, twinkling and sparkling like stars, so that one could hardly look steadily at them."

His second return from exile was permanent. Pastor Bodenstein von Carlstadt, Luther and Melanchthon's trusted university colleague, precipitated the move in a bold confrontation with Elector Frederick. Frederick had had enough of his wandering children. Dangerously, reform was occurring too quickly. He was torn between his distaste for Rome and his precious stash of relics; he was torn between anger at the students and his very apparent support of Luther; he was torn between the demands of the populace and his civil responsibility as a Prince of the Holy Roman Empire and Protector of the True Faith. On December 19, he ordered no changes in worship could be made until the following year. A determined Carlstadt publicly and defiantly met the challenge by demanding that the mass should be celebrated in the German tongue, and both elements of the sacrament would be distributed to everybody, absolved or not. On the day of Christmas Eve, the people responded in tumult with more destruction of religious objects. Then, in this town of only 2,500 souls, 2000 folks sat or stood at the Christmas Day service in Castle Church, waiting for the momentous change. Carlstadt did not disappoint; attired in a simple black robe rather than the embroidered vestments of a priest, he not only shortened the prescribed long-standing liturgy of the mass, but he distributed *both* bread and wine to those present without confession—and—spoke in German! Counter to all he had known, an ordinary man was given permission to touch the sacred bread.

More trouble and turmoil were brought on by radical reformers from miles away who called themselves holy prophets. Adding to the discontent and agitation, they arrived in the public squares loudly preaching only by the inspiration of the Spirit and disclaiming the authority of Scripture and the sacrament of infant baptism. They called for revenge against and death for any unbeliever. Without guidance from their former pastor, the town council begged Junker Jörg to return as Martin Luther. Luther responded to Elector Frederick:

> All the sorrow I have had is nothing compared to this. I would have gladly paid for this with my life, for we can answer neither to God nor to the world for what has happened ... I would ride into Leipzig now, though it rained Duke Georges for nine days. I would have you know that I come to Wittenberg with a higher protection than that of Your Grace. I do not ask for you to protect me ... I say you have done too much ... and you should do nothing but leave it to God ... If you leave the door open, that is enough."

Despite the threats, demands, and certain dangers of the Edict of Worms, Martin Luther chose to walk into Wittenberg in early March of 1522.

V.

Junker Jörg cut off his bushy beard and tossed his noble knightly garb, the sword and scarlet cape, and Martin Luther donned the brown woolen robe of a monk. That same month, his old Augustinian cloister gave permission to its friars to leave their cowls and vows behind if they wished. Several left, and the congregation was disbanded. Despite the dangers of simply being alive, Luther chose to wear the monk's habit, to live and write and preach openly. Once again, his powers of persuasion softened and quieted the enthusiastic rioters. "Give men time," Luther said. "I took three years of constant study, reflection, and discussion to arrive where I now am, and can the common man, untutored in such matters, be expected to move the same distance in three months?"

It was in 1522 that Melanchthon and Luther together completed the translation of the New Testament into the vernacular German for the people who hungered to read it. Luther recalled, "It frequently happened that we searched and inquired fourteen days, aye, three or four weeks for a single word, and yet, at times, did not find it." On September 21, 1522, the first printed copies of the translated New Testament were sold in Wittenberg for 1½ florins. During Luther's lifetime, 100,000 copies of the vernacular New Testament were published. It became the bedrock for German literature.

A prominent Catholic humanist, Johannes Cochlaeus, who once thought of supporting Luther, became an opponent. As the New Testament was being distributed among the uneducated, he wrote:

> Luther's New Testament has been so multiplied by the
> printers and scattered in such numbers that even tailors and
> shoemakers, aye, even women and the simple who had
> learned to read only on ginger cakes, read it with intense
> longing. Many carried it about with them and learned it
> by heart, so that, in a few months, they arrogantly began
> to dispute with priests and monks on the faith. Indeed, even
> poor women were found who engaged with learned doctors
> in a debate, and thus it happened that in such conversations
> Lutheran laymen could quote more Bible passages than the
> monks and priests.

He also considered Luther's language to be offensive and accused him of "pouring oil on the flames," which would result in the certain revolt of the peasants. In the latter, he was prophetic.

VI.

Between 1521 and 1523, three popes played a role in the ongoing saga of the Reformation. Leo X died, and Hadrian VI was elected in 1522. He continued the policies of Rome in a letter to Frederick the Wise:

> Separate yourself from Martin Luther and put a muzzle on his blasphemous tongue. If you will do this, we will rejoice with all the angels of heaven over one sinner that is saved. But if you refuse, then in the name of Almighty God and Jesus Christ our Lord, whom we represent on earth, we tell you that you will not escape punishment on earth and eternal hellfire hereafter.

Elector Frederick, still a relatively young man, was not in good health, preferred to sit alone with his thoughts, and was weary of months and years of calamity and confrontation. He wrote back to the pope:

> Holy Father, I have never and do not now act other than as a Christian man and an obedient son of the holy Christian Church. I trust that God Almighty will give me his grace that for the few years I have left I may strengthen in holy word, service, peace, and faith.

Both were close to the end of their responsibilities in those turbulent years. Hadrian died the following year; Frederick would outlive him by only two years and die in 1525. Pope Hadrian was replaced by another Medici, Pope Clement VII, who ruled the Vatican for the next twelve years.

The year 1523 brought both protection and peril to Luther. Saxony under the watchful eye of Frederick was perhaps the only place in Europe where he had relative safety from the reach of the Catholic Church. He dared not travel further. And so, unwilling to be in hiding any longer, he settled into Wittenberg where he found many changes. Not only was there reform of the liturgy, in which the language of the people was now used, but monks and nuns were spilling out of the monasteries and convents in increasing numbers. Luther wrote in *On Monastic Vows* that they were not special nor more pure and perfect Christians than the cowherd or washerwoman; Scripture gave no basis for such a distinction. It was common knowledge that monasteries were sometimes places of hypocritical chastity. "The real question is not whether vows can be kept, but whether they have been enjoined by God." Some of the monks and priests were even rejecting their vows of celibacy and marrying. Old friend, preacher, and fiery colleague Carlstadt was among them. Luther, however, was not ready for such a move. As far as a wife, he said, "They won't give one to me. Nobody will put pigtails on my pillow!" He did give advice and aid to a group of nuns from Nimbschen Convent at Grimma who desired to leave; his contact was Sister Magdalena von Bora.

Ulrich von Hutten, fervent and outspoken poet of the Reformation and the German populace who had once been named the poet laureate of the empire by Maximilian, lived in poverty and with severe illness. He asked for help from Erasmus, but was denied, and so von Hutten wrote his final *An Expostulation* against the learned humanist, declaring him to be an intellectual preaching only from the sidelines. Erasmus, still a supporter of Rome, once again hoped to settle differences with time and patience; Hutten had no time left. He was banished and fled to Switzerland and safety where he died in August. Zwingli, the Swiss reformer wrote satirically, "Behold this destroyer, the terrible Hutten, whom we see so fond of the people and of children! This mouth, which blew storms upon the pope, breathes nothing but gentleness and goodness." A persuasive voice and pen of the Reformation was silenced.

Martin Luther had had enough time in his own company.

He was ready to return to his preaching and writing and teaching in Wittenberg. It was time for work. The biographer Bainton summarized Luther's philosophy of labor:

> The Virgin Mary worked, and the most amazing example
> of her humility is that after she had received the astonishing
> news that she was to be the mother of the Redeemeer, she
> did not vaunt herself but went back and milked the cows,
> scoured the kettles, and swept the house like any housemaid.
> Peter worked as a fisherman and was proud of his skill,
> though not too proud to take a suggestion from the Master
> when he told him to cast on the other side ... the shepherds,
> after seeing the babe, went back.

Luther's comment concerning the Nativity was, "Surely that must be wrong. We should correct the passage to read, 'They went and shaved their heads, fasted, told their rosaries, and put on cowls.' Instead we read, 'The shepherds returned.' Where to? To their sheep. The sheep would have been in a sorry way if they had not." Luther the monk returned as a shepherd; his congregation and students were his sheep. He has often been quoted as saying, "If I rest, I rust."

This was the complicated man that Catharina von Bora would marry. He was both debater and mediator, confident intellectual and searching student, admired leader and despised heretic, reverent pious priest and sensual earthy peasant. The depth of the man, his logic, reasoning, theology, and emotions cannot possibly be fully captured on paper. This is the man that Catharina would hear unsettling news about, trust with her life, argue and agree with, choose to marry, create a household and home life for him, and offer wisdom and support in times of crisis. He would become companion and dearest friend, academic mentor, fellow gardener, and father of her six children. In the matters of little things and of great things, he would change her life, and she would change his.

As 1523 passed into the following year, Catharina was twenty-four years old; Martin was forty.

> And having thus chosen our course, without guile and with
> pure purpose, let us renew our trust in God, and go forward
> without fear and with manly hearts.
>
> —Abraham Lincoln, July 4, 1860

Chapter Eleven

The wind of joy, and youth, and love;
Spirit of the new awakened year!
The sun in his blue realm above
Smooths a bright path when thou art here.

In lawns the murmuring bee is heard,
The wooing ring-dove in the shade;
On thy soft breath, the new-fledged bird
Takes wing, half happy, half afraid.

—*"The West Wind" by William Cullen Bryant*

April 5, 1523

I.

Nobody knows the actual reasons for the departure of Catharina and her sister nuns from Nimbschen Convent in 1523. They were not recorded, or if they were, the documents have never been uncovered. We can only take the historical facts of the times and surmise what might have convinced several young women to renounce their sacred vows to the church, leave their security and community and home of several years, and, without a single possession nor a florin to their names, walk straight into the unknown. The action could not have been taken lightly. Nothing was taken lightly at Nimbschen.

They did know that they had support from the outside even as danger mounted. It was no secret that any aid for the nuns and monks was severely punished by Duke George who did not look the other way when it came to the emptying of the convents and monasteries in his part of Saxony. To put fear into the hearts of anybody who attempted such actions, he declared death to be the punishment. One Henry Kehner helped a nun to escape from Sornzig and his head was paraded on a pole in public.

The walls of the holy orders were not impenetrable. Broadsheets detailing the current volatile political and religious happenings of the day, poetry with double meanings, lilting songs sung by traveling minstrels melodically telling the true temper of the peasant, scriptural translations in the German language, and even essays written by Luther himself declaring his opposition to authoritarian Rome found their way into the hands, minds, and hearts of the monastics. Some of the banned information was slipped into flour sacks and vegetable baskets that arrived at the kitchen door; relatives clandestinely passed news along during visitation hours. Interaction of the classes at country fairs and church festivals fostered and fired communication.

Questions and doubts and daring certainly arose in Grimma. Persuasion to defect most likely came to the convent sisters from their own familial brothers of the nearby Augustinian monastery in Grimma. Its Prior, Wolfgang von Zeschau, who later became a Lutheran pastor, had left with half of his monks in 1522. Luther had visited that monastery in 1516 and in 1519. The middle class was growing intellectually and financially while gaining confidence. The humanists in the universities aptly used satire against Rome in their literature and helped to make personal opinion and dissension permissible. Although the disintegration of the feudal system offered both opportunity and, in many cases, increased hardship for the peasants who were still obsessed with the Day of Judgment and Evil that roamed the skies, even they stirred with a new feeling of freedom beyond the Bond of the Shoe. Sympathetic engravers placed the peasant with a hoe over his shoulder as a symbolic defender of Luther. The printing presses rolled. The people read. Like it or not, Martin Luther wore the hat of a leader.

The painful story of one nun, Florentina von Oberweimar from Neuenhelfta Convent near Eisleben, has been chronicled. She managed to read some of Luther's works that had been smuggled into her convent. In response, she wrote a letter to Luther and was punished by a month's harsh imprisonment within her walls. Returned to her cell, she was forced to wear a crown of straw upon her head and lie prostrate on the ground as the other nuns trod upon her body on their way to prayers. An attempt to escape failed, and superiors then chained her, handing down the sentence that "on seven Wednesdays and seven Fridays she is to be scourged by ten persons at once." With the help of friends, she escaped again; Luther published the events in his "Story How God Helped a Worthy Nun." Leaving a convent was not a trivial thing.

The man who would play a vital part in the events at Nimbschen was Leonard Koppe from Torgau. This 60-year-old man, who risked his life to aid Catharina and her sisters' escape, was a merchant who often delivered goods to the convent with his wagon. In his earlier years, he had studied at Leipzig and Erfurt, and he knew Martin Luther personally. The names of nine nuns who reached their destination in Wittenberg are recorded. Some accounts add three other unnamed sisters who returned to their homes in Torgau.

II.

EASTER EVE 1523

Awareness of both the frightening unknown and the seeds of hopeful joy filled Catharina with foreboding as she impatiently waited for the minutes to pass on that clear moonlit night of April 5. Listening again at her window, she heard nothing but the sounds of the night. A crisp snap of a branch, the ever-present wind passing stealthily through the tall treetops, some tiny night creature scampering through a wide crack in the wall, a small owl flying with velvet wings as it swooped and missed its target. She raised her head and closed her eyes tightly, straining in vain to hear distant sounds of wagon wheels crunching on the road.

Two muffled knocks broke the silence of the eleventh hour. Catharina ran to the heavy oak door and opened it. She cringed as the creak of the unpolished brass hinges complained loudly enough to be heard far down the dark hall. Behind the door stood six nervous young nuns wrapped in their heavy cloaks. Frightened eyes, wide-open in the illumination of the single flickering candle, dominated their pale youthful faces that were framed by hoods. They froze for a moment with all senses alert until they were quite sure that the squeaking door had not been heard. "Come in quickly!" whispered Catharina. After carefully closing the door behind them, she embraced each one.

"Where are the others?" asked the shortest nun, Sister Elizabeth von Konitz, her eyes darting around the small room. "It's almost time to go! Do you think they have been discovered? Should we go back to our cells? Catharina, it is nearly midnight! Have you been listening for the wagon? Where is it? Where is Herr Koppe?" She wrung her hands in despair. "Perhaps he is not coming at all!"

"Hush, Elizabeth!" said one of the others with a steady voice. "They will all be here. This is not the time to panic." She was Magdalene Staupitz, a girl with a round plain face. Elizabeth, as well as two sisters, Veronica and Margaret von Zeschau, were from a nearby town. They had grown up and played together as children. One by one, as their family futures and fortunes became economically unstable, their parents, who had no hope of financial recovery, had brought them to Nimbschen Convent to make lives for themselves. The new monastic world presented problems for girlhood comrades since the observance of the strict laws of silence at the cloister were expected and demanded. Close friendships were forbidden, and speaking to each other was allowed only at certain times. Neither form nor discipline could muzzle the young women, however; they developed their own personal sign language and communicated far more than anyone else realized.

Margaret and Veronica each clasped a hand of their trembling friend until she was quieted. "I'm sorry," she whispered. "I'll be all right now, truly, I will." She wiped the tears from her cheeks and crossed herself. She was quite aware that there was no turning back now.

Ave and Margarethe Schoenfeld completed the cluster of nervous intent nuns. They huddled in the corner of the cell, their arms protectively around each other. They had taken their final vows on the same day as Catharina.

Ave was the first to hear the slow shuffling footsteps echoing far down the hall of the dormitory. She silently gathered the other nuns into the corner of the cell where she and her sister had been standing. They dared not breathe. The sounds of the steps came closer and closer. The young nuns soon recognized the uneven step-slide sounds as belonging to Sister Anna Spaldeholz, an elderly and nearly deaf nun who often walked the halls at night with her lantern when she was unable to sleep. Blessed by uncanny sight, however, she made it her business to know everything that happened at the convent.

Catharina quickly moved the lit taper from the window, hastily placed it on the little chest near her cot, and then jumped into her bed and pulled the blanket over her head. The girls stood like statues, praying they would not be found nor that their two missing compatriots would arrive too soon.

The footsteps stopped in an ominous silence just outside the door. The latch clicked; the door creaked noisily as it slowly opened. The girls managed to hide behind it as Sister Anna took a step into the room.

"Sister Catharina! Your candle is burning! I saw it flicker beneath your door from far down the hall. Are you ill?" asked the old woman kindly.

"No, Sister Anna. I am not sick." Catharina's voice came from beneath the covers.

"What did you say? Speak up!" commanded the elder nun.

"I must have fallen asleep. I am sorry," Catharina said in a louder voice and in misery because she had to lie to the aged woman. "No, I am not ill."

"Extinguish the light then, Sister," demanded the old nun with a note of exasperation. "Good candles should not be wasted on the darkness." She waited. The frightened hidden nuns did not stir.

Beneath the blanket, Catharina's heart pounded with fear; she knew the safety of all the young women depended upon her. Wrapping the heavy woolen cover around her body, she reached and tried to blow out the candle. She failed. Sister Anna looked at her with a combination of disgust and consternation; the nuns behind the door froze in silent agony. Catharina again gathered the quilt around her neck as she stretched and blew again. The flame was put out.

She fell back into her bed as Sister Anna sighed and said, "You must be a better steward of your gifts. Good night, Sister."

"Thank you, Sister Anna. Good night," Catharina mumbled as the door was pulled shut and the old woman continued to make her way down the hall. The other girls did not move for interminable moments as they listened to the quiet and then stepped out from their hiding place. Catharina breathed deeply, slipped out of her bed, and went to the window, hoping to hear the wagon approaching. "Aunt Magdalena," she said to herself. "Will your plan work?"

III.

Sister Magdalena, Catharina's gentle but enterprising and sympathetic aunt at Nimbschen and her father's sister, had planned the details of the nighttime departure that Easter Eve. She possessed the concern and knowledge that would portend the foresight to succeed. Through friends outside the convent, she had made contact with Dr. Luther asking for his help. He, in turn, engaged the aid of Herr Leonard Koppe. On this night, Koppe would risk his life to take Catharina and her friends from the confines of the cloister and bring them to the village of Torgau where they would be greeted by Pastor Gabriel Zwilling and sent on their way to the city of Wittenberg. Magdalena herself together with twenty other nuns would leave the convent in 1526. Nineteen remained.

On this night of April 5, 1523, the young women suddenly heard rustling noises outside the door and the four taps which were the planned signal from the other two nuns who were part of the escape. Lenita von Gohlis and Eva Grosse entered quickly and quietly just as Catharina thought she heard the sounds of Herr Koppe's approaching wagon.

"Listen. Listen!" she whispered with great excitement. "Listen! Do you hear anything?"

Elizabeth and Veronica moved to her side and immediately heard the telltale crunch of the gravel beyond the wall. With no ceremony and without looking back, they all scrambled out the window, one by one. They ran across the few yards to the mass of tangled tumbling ivy that camouflaged the narrow passageway that had cracked open in the old wall. They disappeared into the world outside where an unknown life awaited them.

Herr Koppe with his nephew, Leonard Koppe II, and his good friend Wolfgang Dommitzsch, the candlestick maker, greeted them with smiles and strong arms as they pushed the runaway nuns up into the wagon and under a heavy canvas. The wagon smelled strongly of rotten herring. Herr Koppe had loaded it with several open wooden barrels that were full of the decaying smelly fish. He hoped that the stinking ploy would deter inspection by border officials. As Catharina crouched between two of the barrels, she thought she would never breathe fresh air again! She wanted to cry out, but uncharacteristically held her tongue. And the wagon rumbled into the darkness and safety of the forest.

A mighty fortress is our God, A bulwark never failing;
Our helper He amid the flood of mortal ills prevailing;
For still our ancient foe doth seek to work us woe;
His craft and power are great, and armed with cruel hate,
On earth is not his equal.

Did we in our own strength confide,
    our striving would be losing;
Were not the right Man on our side,
    the Man of God's own choosing.
Dost ask who that may be? Christ Jesus, it is he;
Lord Sabaoth his name, from age to age the same,
And He must win the battle.

Ein' feste Burg ist unser Gott
—melody by Martin Luther
—text based on Psalm 46

Chapter Twelve

With every power for good to stay and guide me,
  comforted and inspired beyond all fear,
I'll live these days with you in thought beside me,
  and pass, with you, into the coming year.

Should it be ours to drain the cup of grieving
  even to the dregs of pain, at thy command,
we will not falter, thankfully receiving
  all that is given by thy loving hand.

Today, let candles shed their radiant greeting;
  lo, on our darkness are they not thy light
leading us, haply, to our longed-for-meeting?—
  Thou canst illumine even our darkest night.

While all the powers of good aid and attend us,
  boldly we'll face the future, come what may.
At even and at morn God will befriend us,
  and oh, most surely on each newborn day!

—Dietrich Bonhoeffer, Lutheran Theologian
"Powers of Good"
Nazi prison, December 1944

1523–1525

I.

Wittenberg! Three black and blue days of dust, jostling, stench, fear, and hope. Herr Koppe's wagon and its precious cargo finally rumbled and creaked and slowly entered Wittenberg on Tuesday. What an unlikely group of young women! They were weary and dirty, looking nothing like solemn nuns who had lived in an aura of cleanliness, silence, and respectability. The welcoming committee included none other than the reformer Martin Luther himself. Theological debate with renowned academics and long-standing clergy came easily for him; he was not ready for the responsibilities of tending several young women! The man needed help. Luther turned to Georg Spalatin, the chaplain to Elector Frederick saying, "A miserable lot. Their condition calls forth real sympathy. I beg you also do an act of charity and in my name beg money from your rich courtiers, so that I can feed them a week or two."

The next day, his colleague Herr Amsdorf again appealed to Spalatin: "They have neither shoes nor dresses, but in their great poverty are quite patient and cheerful. They are beautiful and fine and all of the nobility, and not one of them fifty." University students were typically quite aware of this arrival from Nimbschen. One wrote, "A wagon load of vestal virgins has just come to town, all more eager for marriage than for life. God grant them husbands lest worse befall." Still needing help ten days later, Luther wrote again to Spalatin: "Don't forget. Urge the Prince to contribute. I'll keep it dark and tell no one he did anything for the runaways."

Did Frederick help? Perhaps he did. As more cloisters reported losses, Frederick in his wisdom said he didn't bother about such things. It is known that Luther and his friends found permanent good homes or satisfactory positions or willing husbands for the young women. By November, some suggested that he marry one of them himself. He replied that he was not opposed to marriage for others, but he was still branded a heretic and could die on any day. He could not burden a wife and family with such a sentence hanging over his head. As the months passed, circumstances were positive for all—for all except one. That one was Catharina von Bora.

Convent life had offered some useful skills, but after sweeping, scrubbing, gardening, and prayers, learning how to manage a household was not one of them. Good fortune shone on the young woman when she was placed in the home of Philip Reichenbach, a city clerk and lawyer with high social connections. He would one day be named mayor of the town. In his home, she learned about cooking and brewing, as well as keeping an orderly house for the family. Her second employer was Lucas Cranach, the well-known artist and goldsmith whose fine home was at Castle Street and Market. In addition to his studio, he was owner of a printery, a wine shop, and a paper warehouse. His guests were the cream of Wittenberg society, including the Elector himself and in October of 1523, Christian II of Denmark who presented a gold ring to her for her service. Catharina improved not only her domestic talents in the great household, but social skills that had not been at the top of the list at Nimbschen. Even so, there was an unexpected turn of events.

From 1518 to 1521, a young patrician from Nuremberg by the name of Hieronymous Baumgaertner had studied at the University of Wittenberg; his chief mentor was Melanchthon. In 1523 some time in the spring after the arrival of the nuns, he returned to the city to visit his beloved teacher. He met Catharina and the two fell in love. A wedding was expected. In sixteenth century Germany, parents by tradition had to approve of the marriage. Hieronymous went to Nuremberg for the required permission; months passed, and he did not return. Aware of Catharina's despair, in October of 1524, Luther wrote to him: "If you wish to keep your Kate von Bora, be quick about it before she is given to another. She has not yet overcome her love for you. I would rejoice mightily if you two were united." The Baumgaertner parents, however, had no intention of allowing their dear son to wed a runaway sister of the Church. In their city, death was the punishment for marrying a nun. They quickly arranged another marriage for him to a fourteen-year-old girl, Sibylle von Tutzing, who possessed a proper and good name, a rich dowry, and respectable parents. Catharina never saw him again. History does not record whether or not she ever forgot her first love, or if he always held a hidden bittersweet place in her heart.

II.

The Lutheran Church has long been known as the "Singing Church." From prelude to liturgy to prayers to congregational hymn singing to choirs to postlude, the services are book-ended and alive with expressive music of voice and instrument. This was not the case for Christians before the advent of the Reformation. "The devil doesn't stay where there's music," were Luther's words. An accomplished singer and player of the flute and lute, Luther arranged new settings for the liturgy so that every word could be clearly understood in the common vernacular; no longer was "Sanctus, Sanctus, Sanctus" chanted by only the priest or monastic choir, but all the people sang, "Holy, Holy, Holy." In 1524, he wrote hymns for people to sing together in four-part harmony as a congregation. Before, the main melody was carried by a male voice, usually the tenor, and others joined in unison. This first Protestant hymnbook contained several songs to be sung at worship services, four of which were composed by him. They included his personal and passionate plea, "Out of the Depths I Cry to Thee" and "Dear Christians One and All

Rejoice." Mid-week singing practices gave congregants instruction, and it was expected that families at home would rehearse the songs together as part of their devotions. He intended that music should be a high and honored part of worship. Clearly enthusiastic about the importance of the art for all the people, his own words are evidence:

> Music is a fair and lovely gift of God which has often wakened and moved me to the joy of preaching ... Next after theology I give music the highest place and the greatest honor ... Experience proves that next to the Word of God only music deserves to be extolled as the mistress and governess of the feelings of the human heart ... My heart bubbles up and overflows in response to music.

Quick to notice the joy and strong communal spirit that group singing produced, his enemies complained that "the people sing themselves into this heretical church; Luther's hymns have misled more souls than all his writings and sermons."

As the years passed, he composed many more harmonious songs for the congregations. Music for the masses thus became an accepted and revered part of the lives of all—priest, patrician, and peasant. Fragments of melody, symbols of freedom and self-worth, became powerful hymns of prayer and praise. Music, its melody and lyrics, has a way of traveling and echoing through valley and village and into the spirit of a people, and there is nothing that can be done to stop it.

III.

All was not sunshine and roses. All was not as harmonious as the congregational singing in the churches and songfests in the family home and town square. Trouble loomed ahead. Serious trouble.

The stage was set for what became known as the Peasants' War.

More than two hundred years later, the American Revolution would have as its rallying point and banner, "United we stand. Divided we fall." That sentiment would have served the Bond of the Shoe well. In 1524 and the ensuing years, many scattered groups, particularly in southern Germany, rose up with vengeance to right the injustices done to them for centuries past. The feudal system and its authority was disintegrating while at the same time, the Church and its dominance was crumbling from within. The emperor was more interested in his troubles with the Turks than making decisive moves in Germany's backcountry. As abusive and leaden as the power of feudalism and religious control was, this left a void of regulatory guidance and management regarding the sudden bursts of strength by the protesters. This also left a dangerous situation for the largely uneducated population that was unversed in leadership or diplomacy, qualities necessary to successfully carry through a revolution—or a reformation. No consolidation nor visionary plan was in place. Idiomatically, there were too many cooks in the kitchen. Accountable to nobody and trusting no man, farmers, students, blacksmiths, and citizens from every walk of life were ready to write history; they carried their own axes and pitchforks and hammers and sticks and anger into churches and houses and castles and schools. They destroyed and debased the objects of their pain, be they man or statue, relic or room. Arbitration or discussion was neither considered nor accepted by those who chose to arm themselves and take revenge against the nobles and the Church in the name of justice. Luther warned that the common man must not seize the sword; if he did, the certain outcome would be "neither authority nor order nor land, but only murder and bloodshed." Because Luther did not support their revolt, the dissidents called him "Dr. Lügner"—Dr. Liar. His premonitions were accurate. The widespread and disorganized citizen militia burned and ransacked hundreds of monasteries and castles, and the bloodshed of innocents on both sides was left in its wake.

Well over 100,000 peasants and nobility died fighting or were executed in this firestorm of religious and political upheaval. The reformers' hopes to return Christianity to its New Testament roots were almost demolished. Historian Macauley penned these words:

> The sixteenth century was comparatively a time of light. Yet even in the sixteenth century a considerable number of those who quitted the old religion followed the first confident and plausible guide who offered himself, and were soon led into errors far more serious than those which they had renounced.

Luther saw the years of nurturing reform go up in smoke. Nevertheless, despite his denunciations and distancing himself from the renegades, many of the acts of violence were attributed to "Lutheranism." Historian Will Durant wrote simply, "The Reformation itself almost perished in the Peasants' War."

One person who felt he had the qualifications and holy direction to take charge was a radical reformed cleric, Thomas Müntzer. He saw himself as the true interpreter of heaven's plan—theocracy—as opposed to Luther who strongly espoused the separation of church and state and a middle road of compromise when it came to Rome. Müntzer had been banned from Saxony, but he returned loudly denigrating Luther and declaring that only the elect should survive. They were duty-bound to slaughter any unbelievers. The elect were the "saints" who followed his direction:

> What courage has he, Dr. Pussyfoot, the new pope of Wittenberg, Dr. Easychair, the basking sycophant? He says there should be no rebellion because the sword has been committed by God to the ruler, but the power of the sword belongs to the whole community . . . If you be only three wholly committed unto God, you need not fear one hundred thousand. On! On! On! Spare not! Pity not the godless when they

cry. Remember the command of God to Moses to destroy utterly and show no mercy. The whole countryside is in commotion. Strike! Clang! Clang! On! On!

Müntzer's cries were not the first nor were they the last of the political and/or religious fanatics whose egos have threatened respect and reason and humanity in the long pages of civilization. History repeats and repeats itself. Thomas Paine echoes this in his work *The Rights of Man*:

> All religions are in their nature kind and benign, and united with principles of morality. They could not have made proselytes at first by professing anything that was vicious, cruel, persecuting, or immoral. Like everything else, they had their beginning; and they proceeded by persuasion, exhortation, and example. How then is it that they lose their native mildness, and become morose and intolerant?

Luther could not retreat nor be silent when the progress and pain of so many brave reformers, colleagues, and unsung heroes were severely threatened by evil within. In 1525, as the carnage continued, he wrote and published a harsh and perhaps foolish tract entitled *Against the Murderous and Thieving Hordes of Peasants*.

> If the peasant is in open rebellion, then he is outside the law of God, for rebellion is not simply murder, but it is like a great fire which attacks and lays waste a whole land . . . smite, slay, and stab . . . If you don't strike him, he will strike you, and the whole land with you.

The tract did not endear him to anyone. The peasant warriors felt Luther was a traitor; the nobles held him responsible for the whole catastrophe. The princes did not need his permission to counterattack, however. They had already gathered and unleashed their military forces, which finally quenched the violence at a huge cost to human life. Müntzer's followers, numbering more than five thousand, were surrounded and killed. Müntzer himself escaped, was captured, and was executed. Thousands were left homeless and in dire poverty. Their houses and barns and villages were in ruins, their crops grew on the bloodied soil, their farm animals were gone, and their children were hungry. Fair or not, for years and even many decades afterward, the Peasants' War was a blot on the life of Martin Luther, remembered as if he had planned the whole thing.

IV.

In the midst of this violent struggle, two significant events occurred in the little town of Wittenberg that would dramatically change the saga of the monk and the nun. Frederick the Wise, the benevolent and sometimes secret and sometimes open supporter of Luther, died on May 5, 1525. His brother John succeeded him. The second event was a life-changing decision by Luther. He chose to get married. He chose to marry Catharina von Bora—if she would have him.

Why would he suddenly step into marriage at a time when utter darkness and deadly turmoil reigned in and against both government and church? Why would she agree, full knowing the dangers for them that would surely lie ahead? We will never know. There are some hints that may give some explanation. Taking into account that most of the conflict took place three to four hundred miles south of Wittenberg, and that any communication or news in the sixteenth century was carried by foot or horseback and therefore was weeks or months in arriving, he may have been unaware of the extent of the terror that June. Even knowing the facts, his weapon was not his presence, but his pen. Then, time and again, he had firmly stated that marriage was a good thing for others but not for him, although on one occasion he did say he might marry on his deathbed to show Rome that he could do it! Another factor was his elderly father. Since his son was a little boy, old Hans Luther had hoped for grandchildren to carry on the family name and soften his old age. He never let Martin forget his disappointment in the road taken from a legal profession to the monastery. It was at this time in the spring of 1525 the son was able to visit his parents, and shortly thereafter he declared, "I will marry to please my father and spite the pope and devil."

Where did this leave Catharina? Obviously, she was an intelligent and reverent young woman, quick to learn and possessing a streak of stubbornness and confidence. With no Hieronymous waiting to make her his frau, Martin Luther, despite his hours of writing and preaching, seemed to take a personal and benevolent interest in Catharina. He tried to help her wed by getting permission from an older bachelor colleague, Dr. Caspar Glatz, to offer his hand and home in marriage. Catharina responded to this proposal with a strong resounding "No!" She replied that she would rather have Amsdorf, Luther's younger friend, or Luther himself even though he was 41 years old! Nobody was going to choose her husband for her. She was quite capable of doing that herself, thank you! Luther was not accustomed to dealing with negative replies or arguments from young women. Was he taken aback? It may be that it was then that Catharina herself made his decision. Were his eyes suddenly opened to the adventurous and passionate and warm person who stood up to him and openly declared her very own soul? His views on women in general were traditional for men of that day; God created them to cook, pray, and bear babies. At the same time, he wrote: "The wife should give her husband love, honor, and obedience; he is to rule her, though with kindness; she must keep to her sphere, the home; but there she can do more with children with one finger than the man with two fists . . . Between man and wife, there should be no question of mine and thine; all their possessions should be in common."

His thoughts were not all law, but also gospel: "I like women to let their hair fall down their back; it is a most agreeable sight." Could she fill a lonely place in his life and bring joy to his father at the same time? We can only surmise. Catharina also must have considered her own age of twenty-six years, which in 1525 was fast approaching an unacceptable age for marriage.

The two unlikely members of this marriage did have some things in common. Both came from pious Catholic backgrounds with several generations of Saxon ancestors. Each had spent many years in a monastic order where stern discipline and faithful obedience to spiritual authority and Roman Catholic dogma were required. In good faith, they had promised life-long separation from earthly pleasures together with poverty and chastity. And despite their vows of humility and their common search for acceptance from Almighty God, the two were honestly eager to learn, quick to speak and to question, and open to taking risks even when the end result was not in sight.

The possibility of a happy union was in doubt, however, when considering their opposite characteristics. She was of a noble background, and he came from peasant stock; this fact alone made such a Saxon marriage impossible. Overcoming that obstacle, monks and nuns simply did not marry. Gossip in the cobbled streets, terse judgment, and sneering suspicion followed relentlessly. Personal differences abounded. Martin was gregarious and lived to communicate with others; Catharina had grown from a little girl to womanhood in a silent solitary life. She had come from a place where cleanliness was absolutely next to godliness; the nuns were fastidious in habit and appearance. He had happily slept for more than a year on the same bed of straw with a dusty coverlet and wore the same unwashed clothing day after day until someone would remind him of the fact. Though he was sloppy in personal habits, such was not the case when it came to academics. There, he insisted that every fact must be properly researched, every "i" dotted, and every question deserved a legitimate answer. Catharina had limited learning, less reading ability, and a library was an unknown place. Furthermore, while working in the Wittenberg households, she learned the value of a coin and keeping exact records of expenses and income. He could not be bothered with numbers unless they signified a chapter and verse of the Scriptures. Martin Luther was a known hypochondriac but did have continuing illnesses that ranged from ringing in the ears to indigestion to heart palpitations to headaches to depression. In matters of health, Catharina was the caretaker and healer; even when ill, she did not have time to dwell on sickness. In addition to all of these differences, Martin was 42—almost an old man—and she was 26—surely with one foot in spinsterhood.

Nevertheless, this improbable couple did not foresee an insurmountable future. Catharina mentioned that it was his eyes that were so persuasive. They were said to be like a falcon, dark with golden rings around; he could not be resisted, and when he looked at her, he knew what she was thinking. She said, "Yes." Luther claimed to Spalatin on the tenth of June that it was not a passionate love match, but at the same time he didn't believe in long engagements: "Don't put off till tomorrow! By delay Hannibal lost Rome. By delay Esau forfeited his birthright. Christ said, 'Ye shall seek me, and ye shall not find.' Thus Scripture, experience, and all creation testify that the gifts of God must be taken on the wing."

To the shocked surprise of much of Germany, three days later on June 13, Martinus Luther of Eisleben and Catharina von Bora of Lippendorf were betrothed, which meant marriage. The public ceremony would be celebrated on June 27. Witnesses to the betrothal on the thirteenth were great friend Pastor Justus Jonas of Castle Church, Pastor John Bugenhagen of the City Church who performed the rite, Lucas and Barbara Cranach who were Catharina's employers, and the lawyer John Apel. Jonas wrote to Spalatin the next day, "Yesterday I was present . . . I could not keep back the tears . . . Now that it has happened and God willed it, I pray for all happiness upon the excellent, pure man and faithful father in the Lord." The groom said of the day, "Who read in the stars that I would cause my father so much trouble, and get into an argument with the Pope and take a runaway nun as my wife? Who told me that in advance?"

When the dawn arose and chased away the shadows over the hills and forests of Saxony on the morning of June 27, 1525, nobody was aware that this day would be most momentous in the history of the Protestant Church. This was the day that heralded the first of thousands of parsonages where the wife and family of a pastor would give comfort and shelter not only to the minister himself, but to countless souls who were cold or lonely or hungry or searching for answers. The house in Wittenberg that the Luther family would know as their home was called the Black Cloister. It was a monastery building that had quartered up to forty monks and was so named because of the garb of the monastics who had lived and studied there. The three-story stone structure with a magnificent carved front door was given to Luther by the Elector with the provision that if he left it, the cloister would not be sold, but revert to the state. This was the house where six children would be born and raised; this was the house where eleven orphans would also live; this was the house that served as a short-term abode, or safe house if necessary, for visiting preachers, many university students, officials, dignitaries, friends who were in fear, and wanderers who knocked on the door. In other words, like all the parsonages that would follow, it was certainly not a quiet place that was only devoted to contemplation and study and peace! Life filled the rooms from morning to night. Its occupants required food and drink, beds for sleeping, acceptance of circumstance, gentle care, and sometimes stern discipline. The wife who reigned over this house of solid stone was Catharina Luther.

And so, on that June 27 morning, guests to the public wedding began to arrive. It was the reformer himself who sent the hand-written personal invitations:

to Spalatin: The rumor of my marriage has reached you … I can hardly believe it myself.

to Herr Koppe: My lord Katie and I invite you to send a barrel of the best Torgau beer, and if it is not good you will have to drink it all yourself.

to a Nüremberg friend: While I was thinking of other things, God suddenly brought me to marriage with Catharina. I invite you and absolve you from any thought of a present.

to the Electoral Marshal: No doubt a curious rumor has reached your ears … I can hardly believe it, still the witnesses are so positive that for their honor I must believe it. Therefore I beg you in the most friendly manner, if it is not inconvenient, help me out with venison, and present yourself.

Many more letters were sent. As required, notice of the wedding and a procession in the streets was given eight days in advance to local magistrates. Wedding clothes were chosen, including yellow boots for the groom—an indication that he might be enjoying the preparation!

And so, on that morning, the guests arrived and, led by five musicians and bell ringers, they made their way to the steps of the parish church for the declaration of marriage for all to witness before the townspeople—women on one side of the street and men on the other. Following the ceremony, the wedding party and guests enjoyed a breakfast at the Black Cloister with men and women sitting separately. After the meal, there was a "dance of honor" which was a promenade and a time of more dancing and merriment in the town hall. The old city clerk Baldwyn wrote, "It was wonderful to see Master Philip dance with the lively wife of Justus Jonas. The dried-up spindle-legged bookworm dancing! We would have walked a mile to see the phenomenon." The celebration continued with a dinner of the Elector's venison and a keg of Eimbeck beer worth "two schock 16 groschen 6 pennies" sent by the City Council. Martin's parents were the guests of honor. None of Catharina's family was present. By town law, there could be no more than five tables seating ten each, and all revelry must be halted at eleven o'clock.

Gifts included a solid silver goblet plated with gold from colleagues: "The University of the Electoral City of Wittenberg presents this bridal gift to Herr Doktor Martino Luther and his virgin Këthe von Bore. Anno 1525." This was a very generous gift costing 23 gulden when only three could buy a cow. It was one of several goblets meant to be stashed away by the couple to be sold in the future when finances were in jeopardy. Spalatin gave them a Portuguese gold coin, and the Elector presented 100 gulden. The artist and close friend Cranach painted their portraits, Martin with dark curly hair, a strong dimpled jaw, and eyes that seem to be weary or concerned about the future. Catharina wears a rust-colored caplet, a high-collared ecru blouse, and a black and rust vest embroidered with leaves. Her wedding ring is on the index finger of her left hand. Unlike Martin, she looks straight at the painter with a bit of a smile on her lips. The portraits are not the fine art of Holbein or Dürer, but they are valuable insights of that day (see image gallery, I-2).

It is uncertain if the original wedding rings have survived. Many people have claimed to own them, but it is true that over the centuries, many copies, some of them very fine copies, have been made. Some historians suggest that on the thirteenth of June, the ring used was that gold band that the King of Denmark had given to Catharina some time before. There was not time to create new rings. An existing ring with clasped hands is thought by some to have been used. The two well-documented rings, now known as the Luther Wedding Rings, were most likely crafted by Cranach, who was a goldsmith as well as an artist in oils. Catharina and Martin wore the rings for the rest of their lives.

Catharina's wide ring, the one on her finger in the portrait, was similar to the rings worn by nuns when they became brides of the Church. They were delicately carved with symbols of the Passion of Jesus. In 1862, a Luther historian, H. Noel Humphreys, wrote in a literary magazine that "the betrothment ring of Luther, which belonged to a family at Leipzig as late as 1817, and is doubtless still preserved with the greatest care as a national relic of great interest, is composed of an intricate device of gold work set with a ruby, the emblem of exalted love." On the band of the ring are represented the crucified Christ on the cross, the spear, the whipping reeds, a hyssop leaf, the dice, and three nails. Also part of the ring is a ladder, a sign of atonement. There are three tiny hearts signifying the misery of the mother Mary. The inscriptions inside the ring give the names of the wedding couple, and the date of the wedding—ꝺer 13 Junj 1525. Some sources write that the center stone was a garnet or karfunkel, a Bohemian garnet which stood for the blood of Christ.

Every facet of the wedding ring of Martin Luther was designed with equally intricate symbolism. It was a double ring, the two rings interlaced so that they could not be separated. Many cultures used a similar pattern. Engraved upon the two bands are the words, "What God doth join no man shall part." —Waſ Got zuſſamen füget ſoll Kein Menſch Scheiden. The initials CvB are on one ring together with a ruby chosen for love. The other ring shows the initials MLD, "D" standing for "Doktor." Its gem is a diamond, the emblem of fidelity and power. When the separate rings were closed, the initials of the two were close together within the ring (see image gallery, I-12).

That day, the parsonage was born. As the sounds of the people vanished into the darkness, as the silence of the stars descended upon the town, as lanterns in the houses were dimmed, as Catharina blew out her own candle, the Luthers began their lives in the Black Cloister. Early the next morning, she who was used to taking directions from others put on her cap and apron and walked confidently into her new life. From then on, Martin Luther called his wife "The Morning Star of Wittenberg."

"Even if I knew tomorrow the world would go to pieces, I would still plant my apple tree."

—husband of Catharina von Bora

Afterward

'Woman can change better'n a man,' Ma said soothing. 'Woman got all her life in her arms. Man got it all in his head ... Man, he lives in jerks—baby born an'a man dies, an' that's a jerk—gets a farm an' loses his farm, an' that's a jerk. Woman, it's all one flow, like a stream, little eddies, little waterfalls, but the river, it goes right on. Woman looks at it like that. We ain't gonna die out. People is goin' on—changin' a little, maybe, but goin' right on.

—John Steinbeck, The Grapes of Wrath

1526–1552

I.

IN RETROSPECT

We have followed in the first footsteps of Catharina in the bleak cheerless ancestral home of the von Bora family where she found joy running and wandering in fields of sun-drenched wildflowers, untilled fields, and deep mysterious forests. She then stepped into the ordered world of the Marien-thron convent where she walked on the echoing stone floors of the chapel, plodded through the dusty fields and verdant vege-table gardens, and brought her strong young arms to give aid in the impoverished and sometimes destitute huts of the peasants.

The next chapter of her life as a young woman took her by wagon through the German countryside where the storm of the Reformation continued to create both fear and optimism amongst the people. Then, it was on to the narrow streets of Wittenberg where theological and political debate was heard on every corner and where she was welcomed into the gracious homes of two of its families. Finally, Catharina stepped with her husband Martin through the door of the Black Cloister, which would be filled with sorrows and joys, learning and invigorating conversation, precious children, a constant stream of visitors, sick-ness and healing, and the love and devotion of the most eminent, honored, and despised man of the sixteenth century. No person can predict and write one's own story; Catharina certainly could not have imagined hers.

II.

MARRIAGE

"Doktor Luther" and his wife lived in the sturdy Augustinian monastery for the next twenty years. Life changed dramatically for both of them. He, in particular, probably found married life full of unexpected blessings. In August of the year following their wedding, he wrote to a friend, "Catharina, my dear rib, salutes you, and thanks you for your letter. She is, thanks to God, gentle, obedient, compliant in all things, beyond my hopes. I would not exchange my poverty for the wealth of Croesus."

Townsfolk often referred to the couple as 'Luther and Lutheress,' and, at times, she was even given the title 'Doktorissa,' a title usually used by people who did not approve of her presence or influence in the cloister. As the months passed into years, Martin called her by many affectionate names in his writings and letters: 'Mein Herr Kethe' (My Lord Katie) and 'Boss of Zulsdorf' (so-called in remembrance of her childhood home and in reference to her efficient supervision of a small farm near it). He also referred to the epistle of Galatians as "my Catharina von Bora."

The young woman trained to be a solitary nun must have surprised both him and the community, and probably herself, with her abilities to run a complicated household. When it came to finances, the words *budget* and *bookkeeping* were not in his extensive vocabulary, nor in the seminary curriculum! She, on the other hand, had learned the importance of managing income and expense while at the Reichenbach and Cranach homes, and Herr Doktor was more than willing to give her financial responsibility. Luther had never found money to be of much interest or value; he neither earned nor wanted to benefit monetarily from the publication of his many books and essays. His professorial and pastoral remuneration from the Elector was quite enough. He was known for giving his coat or dinner or possessions to anyone who happened to knock on the door in need of them. This was a practice that Catharina could not always tolerate. For example, when he gave away some of the wedding goblets they had received, she simply could not allow him to toss out any more of their financial future, so she hid them where he could not find them. The husband reacted, saying, "If I were to marry again, I would hew me a meek wife out of stone, for I doubt whether any other kind would be meek!"

Feeding the family, visitors, and many seminary students who lived in the old monastery cells was another monumental task for her. As time passed, the Luthers bought rural acreage for the harvesting of grain for bread and to feed their animals, including some cows, pigs, chickens, and goats. She planted large vegetable gardens of cabbage, carrots, peas, onions, and beans.

Staple foods of later centuries, potatoes and tomatoes, were unknown to Wittenbergers. Both had been found by Spanish conquistadors and English explorers in the 16th century in South America, particularly in Peru, but were generally considered to be poisonous. The story goes that Sir Walter Raleigh brought some potato tubers to Queen Elizabeth I. Palace gardeners planted them, threw away the roots as useless, and cooked the stems and leaves, which caused widespread sickness; hence their bad reputation. At any rate, potatoes and tomatoes were neither part of the Luthers' diet nor found in their garden. Rice had been introduced by the Moors and cultivated in the warmth of Italy and Spain, but not in Germany. If it could be bought by persons of substance, it was made into a porridge. The bulk of Saxon diet depended upon bread and more bread.

The Luthers procured a fishpond, a widening of "Lazy Creek," which Catharina fished herself to supplement the table. Water was often unsafe; coffee, tea, and chocolate drinks were luxuries of other continents. Beer was consumed regularly, and Martin said that in her little brewery on the property she made the best beer in all of Germany. He wrote, "If our Lord makes pike and Rhine wine, I may eat and drink. It is all right with the Lord if you once in a while laugh and enjoy yourself from the bottom of your heart." And in a 1534 letter to her from Torgau, a town that was widely known for its fine ale, he wrote, "If only I had some of your beer! Have I not at home a fair wife?" The man also appreciated her flower garden and helped to raise his three favorite flowers, lilies, roses, and forget-me-nots. He was proud of the large Erfurt radishes that he grew himself and the well that he helped to dig.

At mealtime, the resident students not only ate the food that she served, but they considered the time as part of their education, and along with the cabbage, they consumed words and mini-lectures when the professor theorized and philosophized between bites of peas and perch. With spoons in one hand and pens in the other, they cleaned their bowls and faithfully scribbled down what he said. These notes were later printed in a voluminous volume called *Table Talk*. Roland Bainton comments about writings captured in the book: "Luther ranged from the ineffable majesty of God the Omnipotent to the frogs in the Elbe. Pigs, popes, pregnancies, policies, and proverbs jostle one another." Here are some examples:

"Printing is God's latest and best work to spread the true religion."

"The only portion of the human anatomy which the pope has had to leave uncontrolled is the hind end."

"What lies there are about relics! One claims to have a feather from the wing of the angel Gabriel, and the Bishop of Mainz has a flame from Moses' burning bush. And how does it happen that eighteen apostles are buried in Germany when Christ had only twelve?"

"The ark of Noah was 300 ell long, 50 wide, and 30 high. If it were not in Scripture, I would not believe it. I would have died if I had been in the ark. It was dark, three times the size of my house, and full of animals."

There are 6,956 entries in all—a valuable window into the casual conversation of the times. Catharina and the children often sat in on the discussions of the men, and she, a woman, was even permitted to ask questions!

A most beloved member of the household, Aunt Magdalena von Bora, who had watched over Catharina while both of them were monastics at Nimbschen Convent, had made her home with the Luthers in 1526. An accomplished nurse and apothecary, she must have been welcome help with all the duties of daily life in the parsonage as well as rocking, raising, and teaching the children. She and Catharina could watch them on the courtyard below from a second-story window where they sat and did mending and other needlework.

The great door to their home through which all who entered stepped was designed by Catharina in honor of her husband and installed in November of 1539. On one side was carved in stone the head of Luther and his motto, "In quietness and confidence shall be your strength. Isaiah 30:15." On the other was his coat-of-arms with the words, "A Christian's heart walks on roses though under the cross." Around it were the letters, VIVIT—"He Lives!"

In the sixteenth century in Europe, the accounts and achievements and thoughts of the girl, the spinster, the wife, the mother, the aunt, the grandmother, the nurturer, the musician, the mentor, the nurse—all of these and more—have generally been lost and deemed quite unimportant in the patriarchal society. Life in the Black Cloister certainly had its sun-filled and joyous days for Catharina; happy sounds of childhood filled the rooms, and her husband was a loving, attentive, and good father to the children. His words: "I consider her more precious than the kingdom of France; I love my Käthe, yes, I love her more than myself, that is certainly true. I am richer than all the popish theologians because I am content and have a true wife."

On the other hand, she woke up each morning to the daily toil of managing a huge household caught up in the midst of the troubles of serious religious turmoil and sharing her life with a brilliant but sometimes obstinate and needy man who was living on borrowed time. The pope was still in Rome in his supreme isolation; the edicts were still in effect. Was the Reformation doomed to vanish into the chapters of a history book? Had he made the right decisions? Luther once wrote, "What if I am wrong?" His music and his children and his wife gave him the strength and desire and even hours of peace to search for and try to protect the truths that he had found in the Scriptures. For Catharina, married to such a man, the ever-present fear of impending danger for her family from waves of bewildering and terrifying disease as well as from powerful political or religious enemies must have made her life unique in the annals of history. But at least, we know her name and something of the fabric of her life. For her and for other women of her time, honor and awe are given.

III.

CHILDREN

On June 7, 1526, a son was born to Martin and Catharina. The same day, he was baptized and given the name Johannes, shortened to Hans, in the honor of and in gratitude to his elderly paternal grandfather whose chief wish in life was to have a grandchild. Five more babies would be born to the Luthers: Elisabeth on December 10, 1527; another daughter, Magdalene, born on May 4, 1529, given the name of her good great-aunt; Martin, whose birthdate was November 7, 1531, just three days before his father's birthday and for this reason was likely given his name; Paul on January 28, 1533; and Margarethe on December 17 of 1534, possibly named for the sister of Catharina's mother, the Abbess of Nimbschen Convent, and Grandmother Luther. Catharina had at least one miscarriage in 1539.

On October 21, 1525, Luther wrote in a letter, "My Catharina is fulfilling Genesis 1:28–'And God blessed them, and God said unto them, be fruitful, and multiply.'" Eight months later, he wrote in another letter, "My dear Käthe brought into the world yesterday by God's grace at two o'clock a little son, Hans Luther. I must stop. Sick Käthe calls me." To Spalatin, he wrote, ". . . From the most precious woman, my best of wives, I have received, by the blessing of God, a little son, Johannes Luther, and, by God's wonderful grace, I have become a father." Little Hans was a healthy child, cutting teeth and "making a joyous nuisance of himself." In 1530 in a letter to his son, Luther wrote, "Say your prayers, learn to love your lessons. May God bless you. Give Aunt Lena my love, and kiss her for me. Your dear father, Martin Luther."

The boy was taught by private tutors at home and graduated from Wittenberg University and the Latin School of Torgau. Thereafter, he studied law and became a court advisor to Prince Joachim II in Berlin. He married Elizabeth Cruciger of Wittenberg, a pastor's daughter. His line extends through his son Nickolus for at least nine generations and three hundred years into the mid 1800's. The first-born son of Martin and Catharina died on October 27, 1575, at the age of 49 and is buried in the Parish Church of Koningsberg.

Their first daughter, Elisabeth, died in infancy. During Catharina's pregnancy in 1527, the plague, the deadly pest, resurfaced in the summer. Her husband had been confined to his bed through most of the year with gallstones, vertigo, and a possible heart attack; she nursed him and fed him his favorite dish, a combination of peas, mustard, and sardines. By August, he was on his feet again as they both turned the Black Cloister into a sort of hospital to care for family, friends, and strangers who were victims of the horrors of the sickness. Pressing the poison from the boils, bandaging the wounds, and providing comfort was about all they or anyone could do besides giving hope to the living and preparing the many dead for burial. Little Hans was among the afflicted. Then, that December, Catharina gave birth to a fragile little girl. She was held in her arms for only eight months and died on August 3 of 1528. Her tombstone reads, "Here sleeps Elisabeth, daughter of Martin Luther, 1528." She is buried in the Stadtkirche in Wittenberg.

The daughter known to be the light of her father's life was born on May 4, 1529; her name was Magdalene, or Lena to her family. Portraits of her painted by Cranach show her to be a lovely young girl with long blond curls hanging over her shoulders and down to her waist. In her fourteenth year, in September of 1542, she became deathly ill. Nobody knew what was wrong; nobody knew how to help her heal.

What monumental sadness and frustration for parents of that century to watch their dear children weaken day by day—and not to be able to do anything! No clinics to go to for examination and diagnosis, no relieving bottles of prescriptions to be filled, no doctors or nurses with medical degrees, no specialists learned in the most difficult situations; no laboratories to find the elusive perpetrator of disease, no knowledge of the microscopic causes of all the pain, no answers, no hope. All the age-old poultices of her aunt, all the feeble and superstitious practices of the doctors, all the desperate prayers of the parents—none of these gave health and renewed strength to the little one. Nobody knew what to do. Lena begged for her brother Hans to come home from school in Torgau; he returned, and for fourteen more days she lingered. As she died in the warm arms of her father at nine o'clock in the evening of September 20th of 1542, he was heard to pray, "O God, I love her so, but thy will be done." Her mother stood apart, overcome by her sorrow, and she wept bitter tears. When they laid her in her coffin, Martin Luther's words were recorded by those in the room: "Du liebes Lenichen, —Dear little Lena, how happy you are! You will rise again and shine as the stars, yea, even the sun!" To the others he said in his grief, "It is very strange—to know that she is in peace and well off, and yet to be so sad."

The passage of centuries does not change the deep love of parent for child. More than 300 years later when Abraham Lincoln mourned the death of his beloved son, eleven-year-old Willie, who had come down with a mysterious disease, he echoed a father's utter grief at the loss of his own child: "My poor boy. God has called him home. I know that he is much better off in heaven, but then we loved him so. It is hard, hard, to have him die."

On Lena's gravestone is the epitaph written by her father:

I, Luther's daughter Magdalene, with the saints here sleep
And covered calmly rest on this my couch of earth;
Daughter of death I was, born of the seed of sin,
But by Thy precious blood redeemed, O Christ! I live.

In a letter to Jacob Probst, pastor at Bremen, he wrote, "My most dear daughter Magdalene has departed to her Father in heaven ... My Këthe salutes thee, still sobbing, and with eyes wet with weeping." The depth of his grief is found in his letter to dear friend Justus Jonas:

> Although I and my wife ought only to thank God with joy
> for her happy departure, ... we cannot bear it without sobs
> and sighs ... So deeply printed on our hearts are her ways,
> her words, her gestures ... that even Christ's death cannot
> drive away the agony.

When Catharina was 32 years old in 1531, her second son Martin was born, almost on his father's birthday. It was recorded that when Martin Sr. saw the babe kicking to be free of the swaddling cloths, he said to him, "That's it! Cry and defend yourself! The pope bound me, too, but now I am free!" Another piece of advice to little Martin was this: "Don't become a lawyer or you will quarrel with the whole world and muddle it!" The boy studied theology, and not law, but as the years passed, he never became a parish pastor. In 1560, he married Anna Heilinger, the daughter of the Burgomeister. Martin, Jr.'s health was poor, and they had no children. He died in Wittenberg on March 3, 1565, at the age of thirty-three.

In little more than a year after the birth of Martin, a third son was born in 1533 to the growing family and baptized in the castle of the Elector. The little boy, named for St. Paul the Apostle, was robust and full of energy. His vitality and the endurance beyond belief caused his father to comment that he now understood why the pope demanded celibacy! The child was tutored in the classical languages by Philip Melanchthon. After the death of his father in 1546, he, his mother, and his siblings were in dire financial straits, and, due to the Schmalkaldic War, they were forced to leave the Cloister and flee to Magdeburg until the trouble ceased and they could return.

Again in 1552, when the boy was nineteen, the family was forced to leave home for some time when the raging Bubonic Plague swept through the town. They sought refuge in Torgau, but it was in December of that year that his mother Catharina died as the result of an accident. The next year at the age of twenty, he married a woman of Torgau, Anna von Warbeck, the daughter of a translator. Melanchthon, ever the good friend of the family, then convinced the young man to get a degree in medicine at the University of Wittenberg. He followed the advice, graduated, and earned the degree of Doctor and Professor of Medicine on July 29, 1557.

He was obviously an honored professional, chosen to be the personal physician to John Frederick II, the Duke of Saxony, for Joachim II Hector the Elector of Brandenburg, for August the Elector of Saxony, and the next elector Christian I. His wife died in 1586. They had four sons and two daughters: three sons, Paul, Johannes Joachim, and Johannes Friedrich died as little boys; the two daughters, Margarethe and Anna, grew to womanhood and married. The fourth son, Johannes Ernst, was strong like his father. He became the canon of Zeitz, had two sons, and outlived three wives. Retiring in 1590, Paul Luther concentrated on the development of several drugs. Fascinated by the possibility of producing gold, he also studied alchemy and was a significant teacher to Anne of Denmark, the Electress of Saxony, who was a rare female chemist. Throughout his life, he faithfully professed the Lutheran faith that his father had preached and his mother had lived, and he died in Leipzig on March 8, 1593. His descendants carried the Luther name until 1759.

The Luther's sixth child, Margarethe, was mother of a long line of descendants. In the year of her birth, 1534, when a deadly epidemic of measles spread quickly through the town, many of the victims were nursed by Catharina and Aunt Lena. Born on December 17 of that year, there is no question that she was welcomed with great joy after long weary months of care-taking. And the family had not forgotten the loss of baby sister Elisabeth. During her childhood, several students and other boarders lived at the Cloister. When they were well, they were fed both food and philosophy; when they got sick, they were cared for. Another dreaded epidemic of measles spread throughout the town when Margarethe was nine. Two of their boarders died, and all of the Luther children came down with it. Margarethe was very sick for ten weeks, but she survived and proved to be a most loving daughter and tender support for her mother. She was the one who stayed with Catharina after her father's death, worked with her at the Cloister and the farm fields, nursed countless patients with her in their improvised hospital during the days of disease, and accompanied her to all the places where she needed to be present. Margarethe was the one who was riding in the horse-drawn cart near Torgau with Catharina when it overturned and her mother was fatally injured. Three years later, on August 5, 1555, she married Georg von Kunheim who was about ten years her senior. Unlike the aristocratic line of von Boras on her mother's side who had faced poverty, the family of her in-laws had survived the upheaval of society. The von Kunheims were a noble, well-to-do, and prominent Prussian family.

Margarethe's death came far too soon in 1570 in the city of Milhausen after just fifteen years of marriage and the births of nine children. Only three survived childhood and lived longer than their mother, but her descendants have continued until the present day. Among them were the Counts zu Eulenburg, the Princes zu Eulenburg und Hertefeld, and Paul von Hindenburg, general in the Franco-Prussian War and World War I and second president of the German Republic from 1925 to 1934. The ill-fated hydrogen airship, the Hindenburg, was named in his family's honor.

IV.

MARTINUS

The final twenty years of Martin Luther's life were spent in his ancestral electorate of Saxony and in the home of his beloved family. His years were filled with highs and lows, huge accomplishments and poor decisions, and awesome public responsibilities undertaken in spite of his wish to be left alone with his studies. Any attempt to tell the full story of this giant of the Reformation in a few pages would fall woefully short.

Initially, it needs to be said that this man was not the thirteenth disciple, as many present-day laypersons and clerics would have him be. He was both pious and earthy, both brilliant and wondering, both demanding and doubting, and he lived and breathed twenty-four hours a day as a sixteenth century European man in a society barely rising from the darkness of medieval thought, superstition, and ignorance. Unless it was his wife, nobody knew his own shortcomings, failures, and fears better than he himself. Despite this, his great passion to give a shockingly simple message from the Scriptures to the long entrenched spirit and freedom-hungry common person overrode all else. Still, through it all, he was just a man.

The remaining years of Martin Luther's days continued to be packed full of chapters in his story. Monks lived among bachelor monks, priests, bishops, and university professors of that century; they did not venture easily into a woman's world and almost never into the daily lives of a pregnant woman nor in the birthing room. Blissfully unaware of the complications and emotions of birth, they played their part afterwards in the rite of baptism in a beautiful and hallowed church as they blessed and smiled at the newborn infant resting securely and gently within the mother's arms.

Nevertheless, as early as 1522 Luther was known for his forthright Nativity sermons dealing with birth. He spoke directly and forcefully to the congregation before him. One sermon, in particular, put reality into the Christmas story. Excerpts follow:

> On earth it happened in this wise: There was a poor young wife, Mary of Nazareth, ... so little esteemed that none noticed the great wonder she carried. She was silent, did not vaunt herself ... Perhaps they had a donkey for Mary to ride upon, though the Gospels say nothing about it, and we may well believe that she went on foot ... Joseph had thought, "When we get to Bethlehem, we shall be among relatives and can borrow everything." A fine idea that was! Bad enough that a young bride married only a year could not have had her baby at Nazareth in her own house instead of making all that journey of three days when heavy with child! How much worse that when she arrived there was no room for her! The inn was full. No one would release a room to this pregnant woman. She had to go to a cow stall and there bring forth the Maker of all creatures because nobody would give way. Shame on you, wretched Bethlehem!

> There are many of you in this congregation who think to yourselves: "If only I had been there! How quick I would have been to help the Baby" ... but if you had been there you would have done no better ... Why don't you do it now? You have Christ in your neighbor ... No one regarded this young wife bringing forth her first-born. No one took her condition to heart. No one noticed that in a strange place she had not the very least thing needful in childbirth. There she was without preparation: no light, no fire, in the dead of night, in thick darkness. No one came to give the customary assistance. The guests swarming in the inn were carousing, and no one attended to this woman. I think myself if Joseph had realized that her time was so close she might perhaps have been left in Nazareth ... Think, women, there was no one to bathe the Baby. No warm water, nor even cold. No

fire, no light. The mother herself was the midwife and the maid. The cold manger was the bed and the bathtub. Who showed the poor girl what to do? She had never had a baby before. I am amazed that the little one did not freeze ... Look at the Child, knowing nothing. Yet all that is belongs to him ... To me, there is no greater consolation than this, that Christ became man, a child, a babe, playing in the lap and at the breasts of his most gracious mother.

Martin Luther—monk, priest, and professor, and now husband—certainly got a full dose of the realities of morning sickness and swollen ankles in his own home. The sacred Advent services and holy celebration of the church heralding Jesus' birth could not begin to prepare him for his own children's advent—the weary awaiting hours and months of his Catharina as she bore him six children in eight years. As time passed, he obviously learned a thing or two and did some serious thinking about that dark night in Bethlehem's stable. It is no stretch to assume that the monk who had become a real-life husband and father, who had lived through the nine months of preparation for each child, could now truly understand what he had been preaching about in his many Christmas Day sermons—how the deep and unknown darkness of the night became hope and light at the birth of the Babe. Yes, the monk, the pastor, clearly understood the perils, the expectations, and the wonders of Advent. And his young wife and family gave him a practical perspective on teaching pertinent and believable theology to his flock.

In the three years from 1526 to 1529, there was something of a temporary pause in the political/religious conflict as the two factions appeared to tolerate each other. Most of the southern principalities of Germany gave their allegiance to Rome while Augsburg, Strassburg, Nuremberg, Ulm, and the northern territories including Saxony, where Luther remained under the shadow of the long arm of the pope, professed "Lutheranism," a name he strongly rejected. However, a volatile point of contention remained.

The reformers were not allowed their religious freedom in the southern Catholic lands, while at the same time loyal papists in the north were legally given full approval to openly worship and live under the banner of Rome. This unequal arrangement was declared in the Second Diet of Speyers. Already known to speak their minds, the Lutherans and the other branches of the reformation movement highly objected and protested orally and in print. Thereafter, they were known as Protestants. When you give men and women the opportunity to think and interpret for themselves, to have an opinion and declare it, to sing their own song, they will do just that. And there will be debate and disagreement. So it was, so it is, and so it will be. The label of protest remains.

At the instigation of Philip of Hesse, a meeting known as the Marburg Colloquy was held in an attempt at political unity and also to write a common confession and communion for German and Swiss reformed groups. It failed on the grounds of differences in theological interpretation of the Lord's Supper and adherence to an unknown future. Finally, the signers included, among others, Martin Luther, Philip Melanchthon who now had hopes of somehow peacefully reconciling with the Catholic Church, Justus Jonas, and Zwingli (see image gallery, I-12). They did agree to give respect to other conclusions than their own. Unity was not to be that October of 1529, and this perhaps foretold the many differences that would exist amongst all future Protestants.

That same month, Martin Luther's little book entitled *The Small Catechism* was published. In 1525, Elector John of Saxony had requested that all churches should have an approved mode of worship. The order of service, written by Melanchthon, retained some Catholic practices such as candles, the altar, and the cross but discarded prayers to the saints and adoration of statues. In 1527, Elector John then declared that the churches and their practices should be inspected. Who better to investigate than Luther, Justus Jonas, and old friend Bugenhagen? The three men were not happy with what they found among pastors, teachers, and the laity. Luther wrote, "The Church everywhere presents a very sad picture. The peasants know nothing and learn nothing; they never pray, and they simply abuse their liberty by wholly neglecting confession and the Lord's Supper. They act as if they had no religious obligations. They have cast off the Papal religion, and disgraced ours."

His sermons continued to speak to the young and the elderly: "Faith is a living, restless thing. It cannot be inoperative. We are not saved by works; but if there be no works, there must be something amiss with the faith." As a result, seeing that education and instruction and purpose were lacking, Martin Luther then wrote two books for use in the churches and hopefully within the homes: *The Large Catechism* for adults in April of 1529; the *Small Catechism* for the youth in late summer of that year. The latter, 𝕶𝖑𝖊𝖎𝖓𝖊𝖗 𝕶𝖆𝖙𝖊𝖈𝖍𝖎𝖘𝖒𝖚𝖋, was inscribed with "Printed at Wittenberg by Nickel Schirlentz, 1529. 15 half forms, 16mo." Its five pages explained in plain language the Ten Commandments, the Apostles' Creed, the Lord's Prayer, and the sacraments of Baptism and the Lord's Supper. This interpretation of the faith stressing the need to "fear, love, and trust" has been printed in the hundreds of thousands and has continued as a guide of Christian education for centuries. "This is most certainly true!"

Once again, in 1530, attempts were made to unify the Protestant opinions with the Augsburg Confession, largely written by Melanchthon and welcomed by Luther. It was virtually a call for permanent separation from Rome and the Holy Roman Empire. Hoping that discussion would triumph over armed action, Luther wrote to his old acquaintance, the Archbishop of Mainz, "It is well known that no one, be he pope or emperor, should or can force others to believe, for God himself has never yet seen fit to drive anyone by force to believe." Although significant differences did remain among the reformed groups, it was published on June 25, 1530, and proved to be a notice to the once impenetrable Holy Roman Empire that the policies and philosophies of religion and relevant politics had forever changed.

It is said that the pen is mightier than the sword. The pastor from Wittenberg could have been the source of the adage, for his far-reaching pen was never long in the inkwell. Sermons, letters, pamphlets, and commentaries poured forth from his desk along with two monumental accomplishments of faith, scholarship, history, and the arts.

The first accomplishment dealt with the power of the German language. In the 1530's, Luther completed his translation of the Bible from the Latin, Greek, and Hebrew sources into the vernacular of the people, using "official" Saxon court vocabulary combined masterfully with local dialects. He must have been a lover of words, and he searched long and carefully to find just the right one, sometimes painfully choosing from among as many as twelve possibilities. He tried to preserve the spirit and rhythm of the ancient translations while giving the Word to all the people, from peasant to merchant to banker. The struggle sometimes evoked humor. Writing to his friend Spalatin, he said, "I am all right with the birds of the night—raven, screech owl, and horned owl. I can handle the stag and roebuck, but what in the Devil am I to do with taragelaphus, pygargus, oryx, and camelopard?"—names of animals in the Latin Vulgate version of the Bible. About this task he said, "Translating is not something anyone can do. It is not just a matter of languages. A man may have perfect knowledge of the languages involved without being able to render the living sense of the one into the other . . . I try to write German, not Latin or Greek couched in German."

His problem was to place the spirit before the letter so that the man on the cobbled street could understand both history and grace. In spite of challenges he faced, the work was completed and published in 1534. Both the New and Old Testaments now belonged to the people. And while all of Martin's biblical scholarship, treatises, and correspondence with the Elector of Saxony were making their indelible mark, Catharina was always in the background providing her famous and sometimes infamous husband with the love, security, and fried sardines that he needed!

In 1534 she reached her thirty-fifth year and was managing the household of family and student boarders, welcoming guests from vagrants to royalty, and caring for six children, the last of them born that very year.

A second major gift Luther gave to people of all future generations and centuries, no matter what language is spoken, is the gift of song. Nobody sings like the Lutherans. The natural-born joy and exuberance of the spirit to make music, the harmony of many male and female voices in a single chord supporting a meaningful melody, and the sheer love of making music together in the church were given permission with the pen and paper of Martin Luther. An author must write; a scientist must seek; a musician breathes music. Johann Walther, the Kapellmeister of Frederick the Wise who proved to be an irreplaceable friend and collaborator in the making of the reformation music, wrote: "I spent many a pleasant hour singing with him and often found that he seemingly could not weary of singing or even get enough of it; in addition he was always able to discuss music eloquently."

Since his schoolboy days of singing for bread on doorsteps, joy, comfort, and praise filled his soul as he sang old German folksongs and religious chants and tunes with his clear tenor voice, often while accompanying himself with his lute that he kept near at hand.

The music of the Church in that century had been performed by the clerics or men's choir; it was very smooth and had little sense of rhythm or enthusiasm. It reflected the sense of being above the people. Luther endeavored to change that, believing that as the birds sang freely in the forests, so should the peasant be allowed to raise his voice in glory to God. Historian Will Durant says it well: "Even the noteless long to sing, and now every voice could fondly hear itself in the protective anonymity of the crowd. The Protestant music of the Reformation rose to rival the Catholic painting of the Renaissance."

In 1524, the first congregational hymnbook containing eight hymns was published; it contained the words to hymns, but not the music. By 1528, a book of twenty-four hymns had been printed, including the powerful "A Mighty Fortress is Our God," which was both stormy and glorious as it proclaimed struggle and grace. Some of the melodies were traditional and contributed by others. Luther wrote both words and music for several, including " A Mighty Fortress," "Lord, Keep Us Steadfast in Thy Word," "Out of the Depths I Cry Unto Thee," "Dear Christians, One and All Rejoice," and the lovely Christmas tune, "From Heaven Above to Earth I Come."

How did the art of music enter the lives of the people? By permission and practice. Children were taught the hymns in school and then scattered among the congregation during the worship service to lead the adults. Midweek rehearsal sessions in the church together with family singing in the home added to the newfound confidence and became the groundwork for centuries of joy.

Not all of the reformers shared Luther's love of music in the church. Ulrich Zwingli in Switzerland preached and practiced simplicity and austerity in places of worship; he forbade all music in the church even though he himself played several instruments. He went so far as to encourage the destruction of church organs and, for good measure, the smashing of stained glass windows. Calvin allowed some congregational singing, only in unison at first, but later permitted polyphonic songs for both choirs and the people. About this, Luther commented, "I have no use for cranks who despise music because it is a gift of God." He also suggested new melodic settings for the liturgy to accompany a German translation except for the Kyrie Eleison still to be sung in Latin. As the Reformation music found its way into the souls of the populace, the Roman Church, aware of its popularity and unifying effect, also printed a hymnbook in 1537 that included "A Mighty Fortress." Martin Luther's name was not mentioned.

In his latter years, a stain besmirched his life and life's work. It cannot conveniently or easily disappear, nor should it. It concerns his attitude and writing regarding the Jews. He put them in the same category as the papists, the Pope and his entourage, the infidel Turks, the Anabaptists, and the atheists. Some Luther critics place him as the major Jew-hater of his time, while others choose to overlook the facts. Neither position is historically valid nor correct.

Martin Luther was born into a society firmly entrenched for centuries in the denigration of the Jewish race. Europe had very few Jews in the 1500's, the result of generations of prejudice, persecution, and downright evil methods of hatred and murder. Why were they so despised? From a theological and biblical perspective, Jews were considered responsible for the crucifixion of Jesus, and they did not accept nor even consider him to be the long-awaited Messiah. But that was just part of the reason for the vengeance perpetrated against them. Often tolerated in cultural Italian cities like Venice and Florence and even acting as trusted physicians to some popes—Julius II, for example, who at the same time also wished to have all copies of the Talmud destroyed—Jews were considered as of little consequence north of the Alps. They were viewed as "different," as arrogant, as unseemly proud of their race, and as acting intellectually superior. They wore odd apparel, refused to listen to or convert to Christian beliefs, and they practiced traditions, rites, and holidays that certainly were not Germanic. On top of all this, they claimed to be God's Chosen People! That belief did not sit well with the general populace. Stripped of their lands and long history of an agrarian livelihood, the Jews were left to commerce in second-hand goods and money lending. In the latter area, they were highly successful, charging only 43% interest, while Christian counterparts either demanded up to 200% interest or banned all usury or profit from interest. Because they were so prosperous in handling money, even the royal courts employed them in high positions, which caused even more jealousy.

Fear reigned supreme. Baseless but convenient indictment was rampant. Rumors spread that the Jews were no doubt responsible for the Black Plagues that took thousands of good

German lives, probably by adding poison to the water; in some cities, four of five Jews were killed in retribution. They obviously deserved such suffering as punishment from God. It was a widespread belief that the unwanted strangers killed Gentile children as bloody sacrifices; they were said to have spat on the host (bread) in the Eucharist and stabbed the wafers causing them to bleed, thus stabbing God himself. To a continent already steeped in darkness and superstitions and great dread of the strange and unknown, the Jews provided a source other than witches and goblins to blame and shame. Someone or some thing must cause evil! And who better than the keeper of morality, the Holy Roman Church and its partner-in-crime, the Holy Roman Empire, to confiscate Jewish farms and possessions, forbid their language, seize and incinerate their books, ban inter-racial marriage, and burn the people alive, if necessary.

The Jews were exiled from England in the 1200's, banned in France in the 1300's, and given the choice of conversion or death in Prague. In the Rhineland, a mob of 5,000 peasants known as Armleder spread throughout the land killing any Jew found. A bit of respite occurred when a great many Jews emigrated to Poland where they were offered some peace, even by the Church.

In 1451, thirty years before the birth of Martin Luther, Cardinal Nicholas V of Cusa commanded that all Jews wear a badge declaring their race. Eighty years later, Pope Clement VI established the Portuguese Inquisition to harshly deal with those Jews who refused baptism; three years later, close to his own death, he relented to release jailed prisoners who claimed to be converts. The stream of persecution continued. In 1555, nine years after Luther's death, male Jews in Rome were forced to don a yellow hat while their women were required to wear a yellow emblem or a yellow veil when in public. Genocide and the horrible holocaust and all the tattered yellow stars of the World War II era in the 1930's and 1940's had their beginning centuries earlier and long before Luther.

AFTERWARD

This was the racist world in the days of the Reformation. Though Luther never raised a hand to physically strike a Jew, never lit the fires to destroy their books, and never participated directly in helping to carry out their death sentences, in his last years he was guilty of his own brand of theological hatred and disgust by using his pen and ink, and this cannot be ignored. Early on in the 1530's, he was sympathetic and wrote,

> If I were a Jew, I would suffer the rack ten times before I would go over to the pope ...What good can we do the Jews when we constrain them, malign them, and hate them as dogs? We should use toward the Jews not the pope's, but Christ's law of love. If some are stiff-necked, what does that matter? We are not all good Christians.

He was convinced that when the Roman influence had evaporated, every unbeliever, Jew, or Turk would see that long years of suffering were a result of the wrath of God; they could close that long chapter in history and now gratefully accept forgiveness and grace promised by the Reformation, the recovered true Christianity of the New Testament. "I think many Jews will be converted."

But they weren't. They were confident and proud of their own faith and its tenets and could not be convinced to abandon the ancient strength of their traditions when the newly born Protestants so easily turned peaceful ways into countless squabbles and divisions. When Luther invited some rabbis to meet and listen to his point of view, they tried to convert him to their ways.

Near the end of his life in 1542, an irritable, frustrated, and seriously ailing Martin Luther failed to follow his own advice. He wrote an angry, insolent, and destructive pamphlet entitled *Concerning the Jews and Their Lies*. It was viciously anti-Semitic, and his colleagues begged him not to print it. But print it he did, and the result was the expulsion of Jews from Brandenburg and Saxony. When it came to the Jews, he achieved nothing;

he added to the suffering of a remarkably resilient people.

Why do we fail? Why cannot the righteous and pure road be consistently seen and taken? Which will be chosen? Actions are a matter of honor versus error, and that is the nature of man—even this man. In the end, the good, the gentle, and the peaceful often survive while what is evil destroys itself. Anger and evil leave immense sorrow in their wake as their legacy.

Martin Luther's life came full circle at Eisleben, the town of his birth, when he died there on February 18, 1546. He was 62 years old. Catharina was 46, and the four living children ranged from eleven to nineteen. Chronic and serious illnesses plagued him for the last decades of his life. Indigestion, insomnia, rheumatism, ear abscesses, and vertigo combined with painful gout and sciatica. He suffered from excruciating bouts of kidney stones for ten years and prayed, "If the pain lasts longer, I shall go mad and fail to recognize Thy goodness." Heart palpitations caused fear for the household, and it is quite certain that he had some small strokes. Perhaps the most debilitating of all were the days spent in the depth of depression when he could not bear to see the light. On one such occasion as a last resort, Catharina dressed herself in black and carried a candle into his chamber. Her husband asked her if someone had died. She replied that when she saw him in his despair, she was certain that God was dead. This prompted him to allow the curtains to be flung aside, and Catharina took him on a wagon ride through the woods, as she often did when he needed to breathe the life and breeze of the outdoors.

Throughout all these sicknesses, she was his nurse, caretaker, and soul mate. Treatment consisted of some prescribed drugs from the apothecary, blood letting, the use of alcohol with amber scrapings to deaden pain, and prayer. The days were bright when he could again play with his children, tend his garden, study the Scriptures, and merrily eat the foods prepared by his frau and Aunt Magdalena. Such feasts did not always improve his health, as he gained too much weight. He was getting old in body and in mind. Aware of the passing days and the fear that all his work had come to nought, he preached the most fiery sermons of his ministry, and his writings became increasingly angry and arbitrary. Historian Will Durant concluded in his book, *The Reformation*:

> He became almost as intolerant as the Inquisition, but his words were harsher than his deeds. He was guilty of the most vituperative writing in the history of literature. And yet his faults were his successes ... What could a milder man have done against such handicaps and powers? ... It remains that with the blows of his rude fist he smashed the cake of custom, the shell of authority that had blocked the movement of the European mind ... His influence on German literature and speech was as decisive and pervasive as that of the King James Bible on language and letters in England ... no other thinker or writer cut so deep a mark into the German mind or character. He was the most powerful figure in German history, and his countrymen love him not less because he was the most German German of them all.

In January of 1546, two estranged heirs of the Count of Mansfeld could not settle their dispute. The town of Eisleben was part of the fief of Mansfeld, and who better to arbitrate than their favorite son and vassal, Martin Luther? This was not the first time that civil authorities had called on him to negotiate and clear up unsolvable problems with his vast knowledge and powers of persuasion. In this case, the two relatives agreed to let him be the judge in the matter.

It was a wicked winter. The journey required days of bone-chilling travel and the crossing of two dangerous ice-filled rivers. Catharina highly objected to the venture and worried mightily about his health. Martin himself wrote on the 17th of January, "I am old, decrepit, sluggish, weary, and cold with but one good eye ... I am allowed no rest, besieged by circumstances

which compel me to write on, on, on, and talk myself hoarse."
He preached one last time in Wittenberg on January 17. Then,
despite Catharina's foreboding, his steely determination once
again won the argument, and off he went to Eisleben on the
perilous undertaking, accompanied by his three sons and Melanchthon. On the 25th, he sent a letter to Catharina:

> Today at eight we came to Halle, but we did not drive
> to Eisleben. There met us a great Anabaptist with waves
> of water and large ice floes that covered the country and
> threatened us with a re-baptism . . . And we could not turn
> back on account of the Mulda—flooded like the Saale. And
> so we had to stay at Halle . . . and took good Torgau beer
> and good Rhine wine. Pray for us and be pious. I hold that
> had you been here, you would have advised us to do so, and
> we would have taken your advice for once. Goodbye. Amen.

The frigid winds blew them into Eisleben on the 28th. The
travelers found warmth and hospitality at 7 Andreaskirchplatz at
Drachenstadt House, the residence of his good friend and the town
clerk Albrecht. The house stands next to the beautiful Renaissance
church, St. Andrew's. He wrote to his wife on February 1:

> I wish you peace and grace in Christ, and send you my
> poor, old, infirm love. Dear Katie, I was weak on the road
> to Eisleben, but that was my own fault . . . Such a cold wind
> blew from behind through my cap upon my head that it
> was like to turn my brain to ice. This may have helped my
> vertigo, but now, thank God, I am so well that I am sore
> tempted by fair women, and care not how gallant I am . . .
> God bless you.

Catherina continued to be troubled and requested that the
three boys and their tutor Rudtfeld sleep in his room. She sent remedies for the pain in his legs. On February 7, he again wrote to her:

To my dear housewife, Catharina Luther, Doctoress, my gracious Lady! ... Grace and peace in the Lord. Read, dear Kate, John's Gospel and the Small Catechism ... Leave me in peace with your cares; I have a better carer than you and all the angels. He lies in the manger ... Therefore be at peace. All your letters have come ... Pray, pray, pray, and help us do things right.

And on February 10:

To the holy, worrisome Lady, Catharina Luther, Mrs. Zulsdorf, Lady of the Pigmarket, my heartily beloved housewife, and whatever else she may be. Grace and peace in Christ ...We thank you most warmly for your great worry which will not let you sleep ... Pray for us, and let God worry! ... Your holiness' willing servant, Martinus Luther.

Despite his deteriorating health, he spent ninety minutes each day listening to both sides and conducting the property negotiations. On the 14th, agreement was reached to be followed by a written treaty the next day. During these nights, attendants wrapped him in warm blankets; on four of the days, he continued to preach in St. Andrew's unheated chapel. Once again, he wrote to Catharina:

Dear Kate. We hope to get home this week, if God wills. God has shown us great grace, for the lords through their advisors have ironed out all points except two or three articles; among them, that the two brothers, Count Gebhardt and Count Albrecht, again become brothers. The young nobles are of good cheer; they take ladies out in sledges and make the horses' bells jingle to a pretty tune ... I send some trout given me by Countess Albrecht ... The lady is full of joy at seeing peace in her family ... I commend you to God's care. *M. Luther D.*

It was on February 16 that Martin Luther stepped once more up into the high pulpit of St. Andrew's to speak. In this last sermon, he softened his anger by urging non-violence towards heresy and tolerance towards Catholics and Anabaptists; they must be "borne patiently and let Christ take care of them in the Last Judgement." But exhaustion overcame his ebbing strength, and he stopped, saying, " I am too weak, let us leave it at that." He felt stronger on the 17th, but delayed his departure to Wittenberg for one more day. That night, determination and will power were no longer a factor. He was cold, had a headache, and had severe pains and spasms in his chest. He was wrapped and massaged with hot cloths to no avail. The apothecary and two doctors arrived together with other personages including the Countess Albrecht. Luther was helped to walk up and down the room and to the window where he looked out and repeated three times in Latin the last words of Jesus on the cross of crucifixion, "Father, into thy hands I commend my spirit." Helped onto a leather couch piled with coverlets and pillows, he finally was at peace. At a quarter to three on that early frosty February morning, his longtime beloved friend and colleague Justus Jonas asked him, "Reverend father, do you die firm in the faith you have taught?" Luther answered, "Yes." And the great mind and heart and voice of the Reformer were still. A mirror was held to his face to test for any sign of breathing. There was none. The two doctors disagreed on the cause of death, one suggesting a stroke; the other, a heart attack. The date was February 18, 1546. Justus Jonas sent the message of sorrow to Catharina.

Church bells began to ring throughout the town. A funeral was first held at St. Andrew's. Mourners filled the church, the square, and the surrounding streets. Led by the Counts of Mansfeld and forty horses, Martin Luther's body was then taken back to Wittenberg in an unopened lead coffin. Mourners lined the bumpy frozen roads, and the sounds of ringing bells hung in the icy air as the procession made its way through the rural countryside and across the two rivers. At about nine o'clock on the morning of the 22nd, the procession entered Wittenberg and slowly moved on the hard-frozen streets and through the Market and finally on to Castle Church where he had posted the Ninety-five Theses almost thirty years before. An unnamed observer of the day wrote the following words:

> The Monday afterwards to Wittenberg, arriving at the
> gate between eight and ten o'clock. The Landvogt rode out
> to meet him and received him and the Counts of Mansfeld.
> The carriage in which his coffin lay was covered with black
> velvet, with a narrow white cloth across it. He was taken
> into the town to the Elstertor outside his monastery, the
> horsemen riding on in front, the gentlemen of the university
> with his sons and students behind, and also his wife, who
> was so weak from grief that she could not walk, traveled
> behind to the Schlosskirche.

Members of the clergy, university professors, and students sang hymns as they walked in the procession. The city bells tolled. Catharina, her daughter Margarethe, and some unnamed women rode in a wagon following the coffin.

Years before, he had requested that one of his hymns be sung at his funeral—"Out of the Depths I Cry to Thee" from Psalm 130:

> With thee there is forgiveness, Lord,
>   And love and grace abounding;
> The noblest thought and deed and word
>   Were else but empty sounding.
> Like those who watch upon the wall
>   To welcome in the morning,
> My soul doth wait thy quiet call,
>   Her self with hope adorning.

At the service, his two close friends who had been at his side through all the thunder and rain and sunshine of the birth of the Reformation, spoke—Johannes Bugenhagen in German and, in Latin, Melanchthon, who emphasized Luther's task of bringing light to the people from the Scriptures in the translations. He also defended the sometimes unrelenting and cutting words and actions of Luther with a quote from Erasmus: "God had given to the Church of these latter times a rough physician because of the severity of the disease." The old Reformer was buried beneath a simple bronze gravestone within the Schlosskirche—Castle Church. It was said that Catharina laid forget-me-nots upon his grave.

****

Never lose an opportunity of seeing anything that is beautiful, for beauty is God's handwriting—a wayside sacrament. Welcome it in every fair face, in every fair sky, in every fair flower, and thank God for it as a cup of blessing.

—Ralph Waldo Emerson

V.

FRAU LUTHER

And so we come to the final years of Catharina von Bora. We have walked in the sometimes shadowy footprints of this extraordinary woman who made an indelible mark upon western history as she passed through the doors of her life in four small German towns where she was part of events that forever changed the story of the common man. She took her first steps in the old family home and flower-filled fields of Zulsdorf and then upon the centuries-old stone floors of the convent in Grimma. Her independent and adventurous spirit took her through the forests on the way to Torgau and on into an unknown future in Wittenberg. In the end, when her life was cut short she was seeking safety again, once more on the road to Torgau. This sixteenth-century woman was a noble but poor farm child, sister, daughter, step-daughter, niece, novice, nun, nurse, housemaid, wife, Këthe (this name of Luther's affection referred back to old German which meant "chain"), mother, gardener, brewer, fisherwoman, friend, companion, cook, Morning Star of Wittenberg, and Morning Star of the Protestant Parsonage.

On April 2, 1546, the widow dictated a letter to her sister-in-law, Christine von Bora:

> Grace and peace from God, the Father of our dear Lord Jesus Christ, friendly, dear sister! That you have a hearty sympathy with me and my poor children, I readily believe. Who would not be sorrowful and mourn for so noble a man as was my dear lord? I cannot tell the sorrow of my heart to anybody and I hardly know what I think or feel. I cannot eat or drink nor can I sleep, now that our Lord God has taken from me this dear and precious man. God knows that for grief and weeping I can speak no more even to dictate this letter. Herewith goodbye: Catharina, Martinus Luther's relict.

She received letters of consolation and support from Duke Albrecht of Prussia, King Christian III of Denmark, and her own Elector, among many others. But such heartfelt sympathy could not wish away the harsh laws applied to widows in the Sachsenspiegel, the ancient Saxon law of the land. It specified that upon the death of a husband, the wife was basically left with three things: her coat, her cane, and her chair. If there was anything left of her dowry, she could also receive that. Immediately after the husband's death, all possessions would be assessed and catalogued and all debts and assets were to be reported to the local authority; in this case, it was Chancellor Brueck of Wittenberg. Any property of the family, real or personal, would belong to the children; if there were none, it would go to the husband's closest relative. Often penniless and ejected from her own home, the life of a Saxon widow was virtually over when her spouse died. She might receive a small income only if she agreed that the state would provide guardians for her children—children to whom she had given birth and provided years of love and care—children she had raised with all the private hopes and fears and concerns that mothers universally possess and understand. Her influence was irrelevant. If she did not agree, the state would control them anyway. The law in its wisdom allowed her to sit on a stool in the quiet corner of the room with her cane and watch the world go by.

If Martin Luther was anything, he was independent and innovative. He did not like authority without logic. He especially did not like lawyers or legal jargon, and he did not like court-appointed caretakers of children, especially his children! Therefore, he took steps to disregard the Sachsenspiegel stating, "I have no intention of making a will. My books which are extant I leave to my children. May they understand that they are not smarter than their forebears. I appoint you Katie, as universal heiress. You bore the children and gave them your breast. You will not manage their affairs to their disadvantage. I am hostile to guardians, who seldom do things correctly." Nevertheless, on January 8, 1542, he did make a will. The original is now preserved in the archives of the Evangelical Church of the Augsburg Confession in Budapest, Hungary. Portions of it follow:

> I, Martin Luther, doctor, etc. acknowledge with this my own handwriting that I have given to my beloved and faithful housewife Katherine as an endowment (or whatever one can call it) for her lifetime, which she will be at liberty to manage according to her pleasure and to her best interest, and give it to her by the authority of this document on this very present day ....

> I do this because, in the first place, as a pious and faithful spouse she has at all times held me dear, worthy, and fine

and through God's rich blessings gave birth to and reared for me five living children who are still alive, God grant for a long time.

Secondly, that she should herself assume and pay the debt, insofar as I am still indebted which may be about 450 florins, as far as I know. There could perhaps also be more.

Thirdly, and most of all, for this reason, that I do not want her to have to look to the children for a handout, but rather the children should be obligated to her, honor her, and be subject to her as God has commanded …

For I maintain that a mother will be the best guardian for her own children and will use such a holding and endowment not for the harm or to the disadvantage of her children, but to their use and betterment, since they are her flesh and blood whom she carried under her heart …

And I hereby also humbly beg my most gracious lord, Duke John Frederick, that his electoral grace will graciously protect and administer such a gift or endowment.

I also ask all my good friends to be witnesses for my dear Katie and to help defend her, when some idle gossips want to trouble or defame her …

Finally, I also ask of every man, since in this gift or endowment I am not using legal forms and terminology (for which I have good reasons) that he would allow me to be the person which I in truth am, namely a public figure, known both in heaven and on earth, as well as in hell, having respect or authority enough that one can trust or believe more than any notary … one should surely believe me much more in these trifling matters; and especially since this is my very well known handwriting, the hope is that it should suffice. Executed and delivered on Epiphany Day, 1542.

Chancellor Brueck reported that Catharina had no ready cash. The itemized estate included the Black Cloister, which now belonged to the Elector, gardens and farmlands worth about 2300 gulden, and household furnishings and books worth 2000 gulden. Livestock included two horses, five cows, three calves, five pigs, and three goats. All professorial and ministerial salaries ceased. The Chancellor tried to break the self-written will by appointing Melanchthon and another friend Herr Kreutzinger as guardians and executors. They refused, following Luther's wishes. Catharina then chose her own legal guardians and advisors, her brother, Hans von Bora, and an acquaintance, Erasmus Spiegel. In addition, she named Melanchthon and Kreutzinger as "assistant guardians" to aid in the education of her sons. They tested the boys and found them to be making good progress. Hans was sent back to the University as he wished. Chancellor Brueck continued to urge the Elector to break the will and follow Saxon law, claiming that Catharina would misuse the estate and certainly marry again. After about six months, the Elector put an end to all the arguments by refusing the pleas of Brueck and honoring the unique will of Luther. Indeed, he offered to provide the family home, the Black Cloister, for Catharina for her lifetime, and he ruled that the children would remain under her watchful eye. The will not only gave respect and legal rights to Catharina and to her children; it paved the way for countless other sixteenth century widows and their families and for western women of the faraway future who would generally be unaware of the birth of their own legal rights. The story of a coat, a cane, and a chair faded into the shadows of the past.

There was not much time for mourning. The Schmalkaldic War took center stage. The Catholic House of Hapsburg, the Holy Roman Empire, was not ready to back away from its lands or theology, and Charles V was eager to turn his attention to Germany. He forged alliances with political Catholic sympathizers, and soldiers were trained to be ready for war. Earlier, the Lutheran states had felt required to unite the eighteen Protestant princes to prepare for certain hostilities and established the Schmalkaldic League. Warfare loomed in the vacuum of Luther's absence. Elector John Frederick I of Saxony and Philip I of Hesse armed and led the Lutherans. In 1546-1547, military conflict resulted in victories and great losses for both sides with the countryside paying the price as the rival troops used the land like a giant chessboard, advancing and retreating strategically to gain the upper hand. Farms and towns were sacked and burned to the ground; possessions were smashed or looted. The soldiers confiscated foodstuffs in peasants' poor larders to feed themselves; many innocent people died. The New Testament promise, "Blessed are the peacemakers for they shall obtain mercy," was soundly ignored by the Catholic and Protestant opponents, both claiming to be the keeper of religious truth and asserting moral superiority in the name of God.

Wittenberg suffered much destruction; its citizens were defiled and their properties plundered. The Hapsburg forces specifically threatened Melanchthon's life and Luther's grave. The Luther farm was turned into a military training facility. Catharina and her household fled to Magdeburg in a snowstorm, returning in early 1547 to ruined gardens and cattle stolen. When the fighting resumed in May of 1547, she again went to Magdeburg where she pawned some of her plates to buy bread. This time when soldiers tried to defame Luther's grave, their leader, Kaiser Karl, stopped them saying, "I have not come to war with the dead; I have enough of living enemies." The grave was spared. Elector John was captured and saved his life only by signing the Capitulation of Wittenberg on May 19. He did refuse to sign the Council of Trent, which condemned Lutheran doctrine: "I will abide steadfast in the doctrine and confession which, together with my father and other princes, I confessed at Augsburg, and rather give up country and people, yea, and my head also, than forsake the Word of God." The Schmalkaldic War ended, but the Thirty Years War that was fought for the same unresolved principles was yet to come. Charles V of the Holy Roman Empire claimed victory for the moment.

Catharina and her family went home—again to destruction. In May of 1548, Charles V proclaimed the Augsburg Interim, which planned to recover the dissidents and return them to the Catholic Church. It failed. By September of 1548, it is recorded that Catharina, despite the catastrophe, had survived and saved the homestead. Supported by her loyal daughter Margarethe, she was keeping boarders who were mainly students and professors of the University, nursing the sick, and planting her fields and gardens. In 1552, Charles V still attempted to gather the Protestants into the Catholic fold. This duly precipitated another Protestant revolt supported now by King Henry II of France, whose action presaged the terrible Thirty Years War during which religious and political factions changed sides again and again as they laid waste to Germany. The immediate troubles of 1552 would not be resolved for another three years until the Peace of Augsburg when the Protestants gained the upper hand and were at last given legal recognition. Within a year, a weary Charles V gave up his throne to his brother and retreated to a monastery.

In that same year of 1552, another lethal danger arrived in the air and carried by scurrying rats. The plague returned to Wittenberg. As the virulent disease spread amongst the people, death descended on every roof and seeped through every window crack. In July, the University students and professors evacuated the campus, and classes were moved to Torgau. Some weeks later, Catharina, who had lived through the ravages of the pest many times before, apparently thought a move was a good idea. She and faithful Margarethe and Paul closed the Black Cloister, packed up their belongings, and made their own way by horse and wagon to Torgau. They planned to join son Martin who was already a student in that town.

She was a woman who had survived a stepmother and a convent revolt. She had challenged death while aiding others many times during the fierce plagues. Long back-breaking hours in fields and kitchens could not stop her enthusiasm to learn and to think her own thoughts. Catharina had overcome sneers and derision with dignity and confidence when she married a monk and many times thereafter. She made a home for that controversial monk, gave him a family, and loved him. He surprised himself and most certainly friends and adversaries alike when he spoke of his marriage as "delight, love, and joy without ceasing." She did not fall or quit or fail when war ravaged her home. Catharina was clearly a survivor in the strictest sense. But sometimes, a combination of simple circumstances can be overwhelming. Sometimes, even a mighty oak can fall in a storm.

A crooked road runs alongside the River Elbe that winds to the northwest from Torgau to Wittenberg. Catharina was on that very road long ago, traveling with her renegade convent sisters in a wagon, the one driven by Herr Koppe as he brought them to Wittenberg in 1524. It was a road to safety. How ironic, then, that twenty-nine years later, as she was riding in the opposite direction in a wagon on that rocky country road near Torgau, again seeking safety, an unforeseen accident there would prove to be her end. Some say there was a collision with another wagon. Others report that her horses were frightened by something, reared up, and caused the wagon to overturn. She fell out onto the hard ground, rolled down into a ditch of icy water, and was severely injured. The driver calmed the horses, and the wagon was righted upon its wheels. She was lifted back up onto the wagon and taken into Torgau to the small cottage of Widow Karsdorfer on Castle Street.

There is a crooked road, a well-traveled dusty road, an oft-remembered road; it winds alongside the River Elbe from Wittenberg to Torgau.

Son Martin and Margarethe cared for their mother for several weeks, but she did not recover. Perhaps she was too tired

217

after all the trials of the past weeks and had no reserves to heal. With the mysteries of the plague all around her, it would not be an impossibility that her immunity finally weakened, and illness claimed her strength. She who had seen the face of death many times apparently knew that her days were almost over, because she distributed her livelihood, her remaining goblets, to her four children. She also gave a family treasure to each of them, including Dr. Luther's gold ring, her own wedding ring, a large golden seal embossed with Luther's coat of arms—a gift from Prince John Frederick—and a cup given to Luther by King Gustav of Sweden. She had a silver spoon with the engraved words *Da gloriam Deo* and the monogram *DML*, which she gave to the Widow Karsdorfer.

Sources report that her last words were a prayer, "I will cleave to Thee as burrs stick to my coat." In her final hours, was she remembering the sun-drenched warm days at the old farm of Zulsdorf as she played and ran in the wildflowers? Was she back there on the steps of the farmhouse picking off the stubborn burrs from her dress? Did she feel the love of her father who was just on the other side of the door?

> O Comforter of priceless worth,
> Send peace and unity on earth;
> Support us in our final strife,
> And lead us out of death to life. Amen.
> —Martin Luther

Catharina von Bora Luther died in Advent on December 20, 1552. At three o'clock the next day, her casket was carried from Castle Street past the Castle of Hartenfels to the Town Church in a procession of academic faculty and students, local citizens, and her family. At the service, Vice-Rector Paul Eber said:

> Katherine Bora is dead. This noble lady was exposed to all kinds of afflictions after war broke out. Outside the miseries

that are many for a widow, she also met with great ingratitude from many from whom she hoped for benefits on account of the immense public service of her husband, but she was disappointed in the most shameful manner.

Melanchthon wrote the following words in Latin in Catherina Luther's funeral bulletin:

> During all her illness she had found comfort in God's Word, calmly looking for another life, commending her children to the Lord, and praying the Holy Spirit to re-establish that unity of doctrine which had been the object of the efforts of her pious husband, and which, since his death, has been so unhappily broken. People were not to forget the merits of Luther, so great no words could praise them enough.

Catharina lies there under the loft of the boys' choir where Luther's Reformation music would resound for centuries to come. Her carved effigy lies above the grave. Dressed in a long gown, she holds an open Bible in her hands. At her head on the corners are the Luther coat of arms and that of her family von Bora, which displays fir trees and a powerful lion with feathers of a peacock. On the border are the words ANNO 1552, the 20th DECEMBER.

> Stille Nacht, heilige Nacht . . .
> Schlaf in himmilischer Ruh,
> Schlaf in himmilischer Ruh.
>
> Silent Night, holy Night . . .
> Sleep in heavenly Peace,
> Sleep in heavenly Peace.
>
> –Joseph Mohr und Franz Gruber

Curtain.

219

FINIS

We have been treading on personal and sacred and inimitable ground. Is written history just an outline of birth and life and death?

> So long as there shall exist, by reason of law and custom, a social condemnation, which, in the face of civilisation, artificially creates hells on earth, and complicates a destiny that is divine, with human fatality; so long as the three problems of the age—the degradation of man by poverty, the ruin of woman by starvation, and the dwarfing of childhood by physical and spiritual night—are not solved; so long as, in certain regions, social asphyxia shall be possible; in other words, and from a yet more extended point of view, so long as ignorance, and misery remain on earth, books like this cannot be useless.

Hauteville House, 1861
Les Miserables by Victor Hugo

Postscript

In a quiet village in Iowa surrounded by rolling hills and farm fields, a house stands next to a white wood church on a tree-lined street. In the house live a young pastor just out of the seminary, his wife, and their small children. His congregation is mostly farm folk, solid people who partner with the seasons for their livelihood; they understand and accept the cycle of life for people and plants from their beginnings to their ends because they live with those truths day after day, year after year. The pastor listens to, ministers to, and preaches to the people. In all of his remaining decades he will baptize, confirm, advise, marry, and bury folks in the congregations he serves; he will mourn and laugh with them, giving his very heart and soul and knowledge to them. Each night, he returns to that house next to the church, the parsonage where he finds renewed strength and limitless love, the warmth of home.

For all her next decades, the wife in that parsonage will be his constant helpmate. She will put on her apron, direct the choirs, play the pianos and organs, teach the Sunday School classes, decorate their living room with lilacs for small weddings, and welcome visiting pastors and missionaries to her table. She will faithfully plant vegetable gardens, can jars and jars of food for the winter, visit the very sick in the middle of the night, attend committee meetings, keep the home spotless, buy and cut and sew bolts of cloth for family clothing, starch and iron his white shirts and mend his surplice, and bring up the children with wisdom and love. This woman will always be there for the pastor who returns to his home at the end of the day. She is the one who holds it all together; she is the one who is both servant and queen in that house. And she is like thousands of other irreplaceable women over the long centuries, the wives of the Protestant ministers, who have followed in the footsteps of Catharina von Bora in her Wittenberg home, the very first parsonage.

My father, like the generations of pastors before and after him, was this man. In one tiny rural church, he met another man, a man of quiet dignity, wisdom, and strength, an aging tall windswept farmer with large calloused hands who had known a lifetime of tangling with seeds, the soil, the rocks, and the prairie weather. They sent me to a nearby strawberry patch to pick berries while the two of them—one who had earned several academic degrees at college and seminary and one with less than an eighth-grade education at a one-room country school—sat on the farmhouse porch discussing topics from the stormy Dakota skies to the causes of war in the world to the meaning of points of theology. Without question, they were equals in each other's eyes. One Communion Sunday after the congregation had been served, my duly ordained and installed father knelt alone at the altar rail and asked the farmer to go before the altar and administer the Sacrament to him, much to the consternation of some of the church mainstays. He said, "This man is the holiest man I have ever met." That is what the Reformation was all about. All are equals before God: the peasant and the prince, the professor and the cook, the pope and the blacksmith, the pastor and the farmer.

The Reformation gave permission to think and to learn, to stand alone before God wearing only the coat of faith. What is this elusive thing called faith that demands personal responsibility and love for others? How could it equal the power of kings? What is this gift that can change history and make a person whole? The Russian writer Leo Tolstoy tries to put it in the words of the farmer Levin:

"Well, what is it that perplexes me?" Levin said to himself, feeling beforehand that the solution of his difficulties was ready in his soul, though he did not know it yet. "Yes, the one unmistakable, incontestable manifestation of the Divinity is the law of right and wrong, which has come into the world by revelation, and which I feel myself but, am made, one with other men in one body of believers, which is called the Church … What am I about? To me individually, to my heart has been revealed a knowledge beyond all doubt, and unattainable by reason, and here I am obstinately trying to express that knowledge in reason and words … I shall still be unable to understand with my reason why I pray, and I shall still go on praying; but my life now, my whole life apart from anything that can happen to me, has the positive meaning of goodness, which I have the power to put into it."

–Leo Tolstoy, *Anna Karenina*, Part 8, XIX.

Despite his century's phantom spirits, Martin Luther ventured to walk out of the dark and declare the priesthood of all believers celebrated with the hymns of dignity. The power survives.

A CHRONOLOGY

OF CATHARINA VON BORA LUTHER

1499 Birth at Lippendorf
1503 Death of Mother
1505 New Stepmother
1505 Sent to Benedicti Cloister near Bitterfield
1508 Entrance to Nimbschen Convent (9 years old)
1515 Last Vows at Nimschen Convent (16 years old)
1517 Connection to Johann Tetzel's Indulgences in Jüteborg
      Luther posts 95 Theses on door of Castle Church
1520 Martin Luther refuses to recant
1521 Martin Luther excommunicated
1524 Catharina and other nuns escape from the convent to
      Wittenberg
1525 Marriage to Martin Luther
1526 Birth of Hans
1527 Birth of Elisabeth
1528 Death of Elisabeth
1529 Birth of Magdalena
1531 Birth of Martin
1533 Birth of Paul
1534 Birth of Margarethe
1539 Possible Miscarriage
1542 Death of Magdalena
1546 Death of Martin Luther
1552 Death of Catharina at Torgau

IMAGE GALLERY

*Portrait of Young Luther
by Lucas Cranach the Elder*

*Portrait of Catharina von Bora
by Lucas Cranach the Elder, 1526*

IMAGE GALLERY

Portraits of Hans and Margarethe Luther
by Lucas Cranach the Elder, 1527

Jan Hus

Engraving of Philipp Melanchthon by
Albrecht Dürer, 1526

Portrait of Desiderius Erasmus by Albrecht Dürer, 1526

Johann Tetzel

Pope Leo X

Nicholas von Amsdorf

Johann Eck

Johann von Staupitz

Luther at the Diet of Worms

Er Römischen Kaiser
lichñ Maiestat Edict wider
Martin Luther Bücher
vnd lere seyne anhen-
ger Enthalter vnd
nachuolger vnnd
Etlich annder
schmeliche sch
rifften. Auch
Gesetz der
Drucke-
rey.

Title portion of facsimile of the Edict of Worms, 8 May (1521)

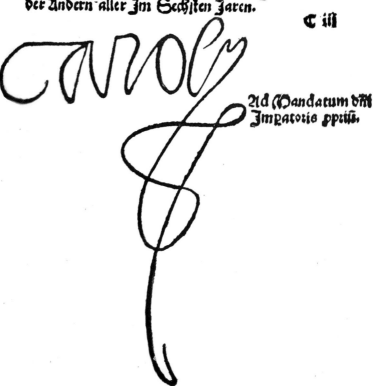

Darnach wysse sich Menigtlich zurichten.
Vnd damit dem Allem volziehunng beschehe.vnd Glauben gegeben werde. So haben Wir disen Brief mit vn-
serm Kayserlichen Jnnsigel Besigelt. Der gegeben ist
Jn vnnser vnnd des Hayligen Reichs Stat Wurmbs-
Am Achten tag des Monets May. Nach Christi ge-
burt.Fünffzehenhundert vnnd Jm Einundzweinzigi-
sten. Vnnserer Reiche des Römischen Jm Andern vnd
der Andern aller Jm Sechsten Jaren.

C ist

CAROL

Ad Mandatum dm
Jmpratoris pprm.

*Facsimile of the conclusion of the Edict of Worms
with signature of Emperor Charles*

I-9

*Emperor Charles V
as painted by P. A. Labouchere*

*Portrait of Frederick III
of Saxony by Lucas Caranach
the Elder, circa 1532*

IMAGE GALLERY

*Portrait of Martin Luther as Junker Jörg
by Lucas Cranach the Elder, 1521*

A view of Wartburg Castle

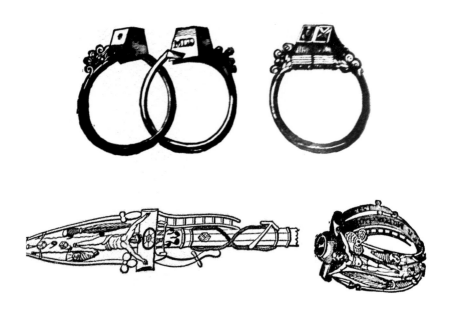

The Luther rings

Three signatures of participants in the Marburg Colloquy.
From top: Martin Luther, Justus Jonas, Philip Melanchthon

IMAGE GALLERY

A view of the Luther House in Wittenberg

Portrait of Magdalena Luther by Lucas Cranach the Elder

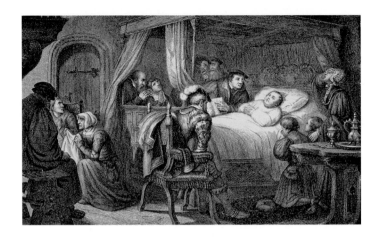

Luther on his deathbed

Luther after death

Catharina von Bora as painted by Cranach in Nuremberg

Catharina von Bora as painted by Barnabas Sears

IMAGE CREDITS

Frontispiece: Map of Luther land From the *Life of Luther*. Philadelphia: American Sunday School Union, 1850.

I-2   **Young Luther From painting by Lucas Cranach** Reproduced under Wikimedia Commons public domain license in the United States.

I-2   **Catherina von Bora** Reproduced under Wikimedia Commons public domain license in the United States.

I-3   **Hans and Margarethe Luther** Reproduced under Wikimedia Commons public domain license in the United States.

I-4   **Jan Huss** Reproduction copyright © iStock/GeorgiosArt.

I-4   **Philipp Melanchthon** Reproduced under Wikimedia Commons public domain license in the United States.

I-4   **Desiderius Erasmus of Rotterdam** Reproduced under Wikimedia Commons public domain license in the United States.

I-5   **Johann Tetzel** A faithful photographic reproduction of a two-dimensional, public domain work of art. Reproduced under Wikimedia Commons public domain license in the United States.

I-5   **Pope Leo X** Detail from a portrait by Raphael of Pope Leo X and his cousins. Reproduced under Wikimedia Commons public domain license in the United States.

I-6   **Nicholas von Amsdorf** Reproduced from a photo of an old woodcut pictured in *Martin Luther* by Julius Köstlin. New York: Charles Scribner's Sons, 1913.

I-6   **Johann Maier von Eck** Reproduced under Wikimedia Commons public domain license in the United States.

I-6   **Johann von Staupitz** Reproduction copyright © 123RF.com/petervick167.

I-7   **Luther at the Diet of Worms** Reproduced from painting by P. A. Labouchere in *History of the Reformation in the Sixteenth Century* by J. H. Merle D'Aubigné. New York: Putnam and Sons, 1872.

I-8 Facsimile of part of the Edict of Worms, 8 May (1521), including title. Reproduced from an image in *Martin Luther* by Julius Köstlin. New York: Charles Scribner's Sons, 1913.

I-9 Facsimile of part of the Edict of Worms, 8 May (1521), including title. Reproduced from an image in *Martin Luther* by Julius Köstlin. New York: Charles Scribner's Sons, 1913.

I-10 Charles V Reproduced from painting by P. A. Labouchere in *History of the Reformation in the Sixteenth Century* by J. H. Merle D'Aubigné. New York: Putnam and Sons, 1872.

I-10 Frederick III of Saxony Reproduced under Wikimedia Commons public domain license in the United States.

I-11 Junker Jörg Reproduced under Wikimedia Commons public domain license in the United States.

I-11 Wartburg Castle Reproduced from painting by P. A. Labouchere in *History of the Reformation in the Sixteenth Century* by J. H. Merle D'Aubigné. New York: Putnam and Sons, 1872.

I-12 The Luther Rings Reproduced from an image in *Martin Luther* by Julius Köstlin. New York: Charles Scribner's Sons, 1911, p. 334.

I-12 Three signatures Reproduced from an image in *Martin Luther* by Julius Köstlin. New York: Charles Scribner's Sons, 1911, p. 397.

I-13 The Luther House Reproduced from an illustration pictured in *Martin Luther* by Julius Köstlin. New York: Charles Scribner's Sons, 1913.

I-13 Magdalena Luther Reproduced under Wikimedia Commons public domain license in the United States.

I-14 Luther on deathbed Reproduced from painting by P. A. Labouchere in *History of the Reformation in the Sixteenth Century* by J. H. Merle D'Aubigné. New York: Putnam and Sons, 1872.

I-14 Luther in death Reproduction of a picture ascribed to Cranach as found in *Martin Luther* by Julius Köstlin. New York: Charles Scribner's Sons, 1913.

I-15 Catharina von Bora Reproduced from an image in *Martin Luther: The Hero of the Reformation* by Henry Eyster Jacobs. New York: G. P. Putnam's Sons, 1890, p. 267.

I-16 Catharina von Bora Reprduced from a portrait by Barnabas Sears in *Life of Luther*. Philadelphia: American Sunday School Union, 1850.

A CHRONOLOGY
OF MARTIN LUTHER

1483   Birth & baptism in Eisleben (fief of the Count of Mansfeld)
1484   Move to Mansfeld
1486   Elector Frederick the Wise born
1497   School at Magdeburg; Philipp Melanchthon born
1498   Attends Latin school at Eisenach
1501   Student at Erfurt University
1502   Bachelor of Arts degree
1505   Master of Arts degree; begins study of law
        Life-changing experience in lightning storm
        Enters Black Cloister of the Augustinian Hermits in Erfurt
1506   Vows of initiation as St. Augustinian monk
1507   Ordained as a priest; assigned to study theology at Erfurt
1508   Joins Wittenberg University faculty; lectures in philosophy and biblical studies
1509   Earns theological degree and returns to Erfurt as lecturer
1510   Pilgrimage to Rome
1512   Doctor of Theology degree; appointed Professor of Biblical Studies at Wittenberg
1513   Begins teaching the Psalms
1514   Preacher at St. Mary's Church
1515   Professor at University of Wittenberg and district vicar of ten Augustinian cloisters

A CHRONOLOGY OF MARTIN LUTHER

1517 Plenary indulgence of Pope Leo X; Johann Tetzel sells indulgences
Luther posts 95 Theses on Castle Church in Wittenberg
1518 Interrogation by Cajetan
1519 Charles V named emperor; debate with Eck in Leipzig
1520 Bull "Exsurge Domini" of excommunication issued against Luther
Burning of his books at Cologne
Luther and students burn the papal Bull at Wittenberg
1521 Luther excommunicated in January
His defense at the Diet of Worms; Luther found guilty of heresy
Hidden sojourn at Wartburg Castle as Junker Jörg
Edict of Worms issued
Many monks leave Wittenberg cloister
New Testament translation begun
1522 Return to Wittenberg
New Testament published in German (the September Testament)
New pope: Hadrian VI
Several clerics marry
1523 Burning of first Reformation martyrs in Brussels
New pope: Clement VII
1525 Betrothal and marriage to Catharina von Bora
1527 "A Mighty Fortress" published and sung by congregations
1534 First complete edition of Luther's Bible published
1546 Death at Eisleben on February 18

LITERARY EXCERPTS aɴd END NOTES

p. 163   Bonhoeffer, Dietrich, *Letters and Papers from Prison*, edited by Eberhard Bethge, Macmillan Publishing Company, Inc., New York NY, 1953.

p. 35   Bronte, Emily, "Will the Day be Bright or Cloudy", *Collected Poems*, 1845.

p. 155   Bryant, William Cullen, "The West Wind", *Collected Poems*, D. Appleton & Company, New York, NY, 1885.

p. X   Chief Joseph of Nez Perce Tribe.

p. 210   Emerson, Ralph Waldo, "Wisdom of the Harvard Classics", Volume 36, Beverly Hills, CA, 1961.

p. 220   Hugo, Victor, *Preface to Les Miserables* at Hauteville House, translation by Lascelles Wraxall, The Heritage Press, New York, NY, 1938.

p. 154   Lincoln, Abraham, "Message to Congress in Special Session"; *The Literary Works of Abraham Lincoln*, Heritage Press, New York, NY, 1942.

p. 219   Mohr, Joseph and Gruber, Franz, *Silent Night*, Oberndorf, Austria, December 24, 1818.

p. 1   Shakespeare, William, *As You Like It* Act II, Scene VII, 1599.

p. 59   Shakespeare, William, *The Winter's Tale* Act IV Scene IX, 1609.

p. 181   Steinbeck, John, *The Grapes of Wrath*, The Viking Press, New York, NY 1939.

p. 223   Tolstoy, Leo, *Anna Karenina*, 1878, English translation by The Easton Press, Norwalk, CT, 1975.

END NOTES

Many quotations are found in multiple sources. Words and sentence patterns, while giving the same meaning, can be slightly different depending upon the translator.

PROLOGUE

p. 5   "I speak Spanish to . . . " . Jeff Kacirk, *Forgotten English*, September 9, p. 245.

END NOTES

p. 7   "There was, then ...", Lord Thomas Babington Macauley, *The History of England*, pp. 49-50.

p. 7   "The whole church might . . .", Will Durant, *The Reformation*, p. 7.

p. 8   "that the successor of the Apostles . . .", Ibid.

p. 8   "There are shocking ...", Will Durant, *The Reformation*, p. 282, 285.

p. 8   "pagan, oppressor, liar, traitor . . .", Ibid., p. 10.

p. 9   "Had the religion ...", Machiavelli, iii.I, Modern Library.

p. 13   "He makes the sacraments ...", Roland Bainton, *Here I Stand*, p. 189.

CHAPTER ONE

p. 26   "It is no small remedy ..."Johann Jacob Wecker, *Secrets of Art & Nature* I-XVIII.

CHAPTER SIX

p. 61   "The wine was knocked ..." Keith Moxey, *Peasants, Warriors, & Wives*, p. 45.

p. 61   "There's naught ...", Ibid., p. 47.

p. 62   "Peasants and their ...", Ibid., p. 46.

p. 64   "A bad woman ... Ibid., pp. 105, 108.

p. 64   "Take a wife ...", Ibid., p. 109.

p. 64   "Go ahead and act ...", Ibid., p. 117.

CHAPTER SEVEN

p. 82   "Childbirth is an ordeal ...", Donald Kagan, *The Western Heritage*, p. 246. Ninth Edition, p. 382.

CHAPTER EIGHT

pp. 88   "I absolve thee...", Will Durant, *The Reformation*, p. 338.

pp. 93-97   "Listen now...", Roland Bainton, *Here I Stand*, p. 78 (See *Dokumente zu Luthers Entwicklung* and *Dokumente zum Ablasstreit*, pp. 125-26 (W. Kohler).

p. 98   "As soon as...", Gretzschel, Babovic, Ellert, & Verlaag, *In Martin Luther's Footsteps*, p. 37.

pp. 102-04   "When our Lord and Master ...", www.spurgeon.org/phil/history/95theses.htm.

CHAPTER NINE

p. 105   "I commit my soul ...", John Forster, *The Life of Charles Dickens, The Illustrated Edition*, p. 498.

p. 105   "Within three weeks..." Edith Simon, *The Reformation*, Great Ages of Man Series. Time/Life, p. 40.

p. 106   "Brother Martin has...", Gretzschel, Babovic, Ellert, & Verlag, *In Martin Luther's Footsteps*, p. 37.

p. 106   "Luther is...", Edith Simon, *Luther Alive*, p. 142.

p. 106   "A simple friar who...", Edith Simon, Great Ages of Man, *The Reformation*, Time/Life, p. 43.

p. 106   "I do not wish to...", Gustav Just, *Life of Luther*, p. 52.

p. 106   "Poor monk, thou...", JH Merle D'Aubigne, *History of the Great Reformation*, p. 82.

pp. 106-07   "Christians should be...", Ibid., p. 87.

p. 108   "Aha! He'll do it..." Gustav Just, *Life of Luther*, p. 49.

p. 108   "My dear Brother...", Ibid.

p. 108   "Take care of...", WIll Durant, *The Reformation*, p. 347.

p. 108   "Truly the yoke...", Ibid., p. 284.

p. 108   "Erasmus belonged...", Ibid. John Acton, *Lectures on Modern History*, p. 437.

p. 109   "To rebel against...", Will Durant, *The Reformation*, p. 165.

p. 110   "Come in front...", Ibid., p. 167.

p. 110   "who could write so powerfully...", Ibid., p. 343.

p. 110   "I despise the pope...", Ibid., p. 328.

p. 111   "If I had...", Ibid.

p. 111   "The contrast...", Ibid., p. 329.

p. 112   "My parents, at first...", Gustav Just, *Life of Luther*, p. 27.

p. 112   "My father once chastised...", Ibid.

p. 112   "From youth I was trained...", Ibid., p. 28.

p. 114   "There is nothing...", Ibid., p. 342.

p. 115   "Ich will ein...", Merle Severy, "The World of Martin Luther," *National Geographic* 164:4, p. 434.

p. 116   "I was a good monk...", Roland Bainton, *Here I Stand*, p. 45.

p. 117   "When I celebrated...", Gretzschel, Babovic, Ellert, & Verlag, *In Martin Luther's Footsteps*, p. 26.

p. 120   "...a poor, insignificant...", Will Durant, *The Reformation*, p. 344.

p. 121   "These passages...", Merle Severy, "The World of Luther," *National Geographic*, 164.4, p. 438.

p. 121   "...would only make...", JH Merle D'Aubigne, *The History of the Great Reformation*, p. 63.

p. 124   "Beloved son, the apostolic...", Roland Bainton, *Here I Stand*, p. 104.

p. 125   "We are sure that ...", Gretzschel, Babovic, Ellert, & Verlag, *In Martin Luther's Footsteps*, p. 49.

p. 126   "... that child of Satan ...", Roland Bainton, *Here I Stand*, p. 104.

p. 126   "Beloved son, the most holy ...", Ibid.

p. 128   "Old institutions ...", Will Durant, *The Reformation*, p. 430.

p. 128   "Martin is of ...", Julius Köstlin, *Martin Luther*, p. 139.

p. 129   "I see that ...",Roland Bainton, *Here I Stand*, p. 114.

p. 130   "The unity of ...", Ibid.

p. 130   "... because no believing ...", Ibid., p. 116.

p. 130   "I will tell you straight ...", Ibid., p. 119.

p. 130   "At any rate, ...", Ibid.

p. 130   "We are all Hussites ...", Ibid., p. 120.

CHAPTER TEN

p. 135   "Arise, O Lord, and ...", Roland Bainton, *Here I Stand*, p. 147.

p. 136   "Some have estimated ...", Will Durant, *The Reformation*, p. 353.

p. 137   "marriage between believers ...", Ibid., p. 354-55.

p. 137   "... unless I am deceived ...", Ibid., p. 356.

p. 137   "The tree bears ...", Ibid.

p. 137   "I look upon you ...", Roland Bainton, *Here I Stand*, p. 164.

p. 138-39   "John Eck, professor ...", Ibid., p. 158.

p. 139   "The inclemency of this bull ...", Edith Simon, *Life of Luther*, p. 141.

p. 139   "O God, Luther's books ...", Ibid., p. 160.

p. 140   "Since they have ...",Ibid., p. 166.

p. 140   "After I left ...", Ibid.

p. 141   "It is a dream ...", Oliver Huckel, *Richard Wagner*, p. 95.

p. 142   "Worms is a ...", John Forster, *The Life of Charles Dickens, The Illustrated Edition*, p. 237.

p. 142   "All Germany is up ...", Will Durant, *The Reformation*, p. 359.

p. 143   "Are these words ...", JH Merle D'Aubigne, *History of the Great Reformation*, p. 200.

p. 144   "Since your Majesty ...", Roland Bainton, *Here I Stand*, p. 185.

p. 144   "After having heard ...", Ibid., p. 186.

p. 144   "one and all not to house...", Gretzschel, Babovic, Ellert, & Verlag, *In Martin Luther's Footsteps*, p. 61.

p. 145   "We have labored ...", Roland Bainton, *Here I Stand*, p. 189.

p. 145   "I know not ...", Gretzschel, Babovic, Ellert, & Verlag, *In Martin Luther's Footsteps*, p. 66.

p. 147   "The very letters ...", Edith Simon, *Luther Alive*, pp. 289-90.

p. 147	"one thing about..." Ibid.
p. 147	"I don't want to...Ibid., p. 292.
p. 147-48	"Violence will only..."Roland Bainton, *Here I Stand*, p. 206.
p. 149	"All the sorrow...", Ibid., pp. 211-12.
p. 149-50	"Give men time...", Ibid., p. 214.
p 150	"It frequently...", Gustav Just, *Life of Luther*, p. 77.
p. 150	"Luther's New Testament..." Ibid., p. 79.
p. 151	"...Separate yourself...",Roland Bainton, *Here I Stand*, p. 250.
p. 151	"Holy Father...", Ibid., p. 251.
p. 152	"They won't give..."JH Merle D'Aubigne, *History of the Great Reformation*, p. 263.
p. 152	"Behold this...", Will Durant, *The Reformation*, p. 427.
p. 153	"The Virgin Mary...", Roland Bainton, *Here I Stand*, p. 234.
p. 153	"Surely that must...", Edith Simon, *The Reformation*, Great Ages of Man Series. Time/Life, p. 179.
p. 153	"If I rest...", Ibid.

CHAPTER TWELVE

p. 164	"A miserable lot...", William Dallmann, DD, *Kate Luther*, p. 6.
p. 164	"They have neither...", Ibid.
p. 164	"A wagon load...", Roland Bainton, *Here I Stand*, p. 286-87.
p. 164	"Don't forget...", William Dallmann, DD, *Kate Luther*, p. 7.
p. 166	"If you wish...", Clara Dentler, *Katherine Luther of the Wittenberg Parsonage*, p. 10.
p. 167	"Music is...", Paul Nettl, *Luther and Music*, p. 341.
p. 167	"...the people sing...", Gustav Just, *Life of Luther*, p. 82.
p. 169	"The sixteenth century...", Lord Thomas Macauley, *The History of England*, p. 50.
p. 169-70	"What courage has...", Roland Bainton, *Here I Stand*, p. 278.
p. 170	"All religions...", Thomas Paine, *Rights of Man Part the First*, p. 57.
p. 170	"If the peasant...", Roland Bainton, *Here I Stand*, p. 280.
p. 172	"The wife should...", Will Durant, *The Reformation*, p. 416.
p. 173	"I like women...", Ibid.
p. 174	"Don't put off...", Roland Bainton, *Here I Stand*, p. 288-89.
p. 174-75	"Yesterday I was...", William Dallmann, DD, *Kate Luther*, p. 16.
p. 175	"Who read in..", Gretzschel, Babovic, Ellert, & Verlag, *In Martin Luther's Footsteps*, p. 77.
p. 176	"The rumor of...", Roland Bainton, *Here I Stand*, p. 289.
p. 176	"My Lord Katie and I...", Ibid., p. 290.

END NOTES

p. 176 "While I was thinking . . . ", Ibid.

p. 176 "No doubt a curious rumor . . . ", William Dallman, DD, *Kate Luther*, p. 18.

p. 177 "It was wonderful to see . . . ", Ibid., p. 20.

AFTERWARD

p. 182 "Catharina, my dear rib . . . ", William Dallmann, DD, *Kate Luther*, p. 38.

p. 183 "If I were to marry again . . . ", Edith Simon, *Luther Alive*, p. 336.

p. 184 "If our Lord . . . ", William Dallmann, DD, *Kate Luther*, p. 35.

p. 184 "If only I had . . . ", Ibid.

p. 185 "Printing is . . . " Martin Luther, *Table Talk*.

p. 187 "My Catharina is . . . ", Roland Bainton, *Here I Stand*, p. 293.

p. 187 "My dear Këthe . . . ", Edith Simon, *Luther Alive*, p. 334.

p. 187 ". . . From the most precious . . . " William Dallman, DD, *Kate Luther*, p. 38.

p. 187-88 ". . . making a joyous nuisance . . . ", Edith Simon, *Luther Alive*, p. 334.

p. 188 "Say your prayers . . . ", Gustav Just, *Life of Luther*, p. 86.

p. 189 "Dear little Lena . . . ", Ibid., p. 88.

p. 190 "I, Luther's Daughter . . . ", Ibid.

p. 190 "Although I and my wife . . . ", Julius Köstlin, Martin Luther, p. 545.

p. 190 "That's it! Cry and defend . . . ", William Dallman, DD, *Kate Luther*, p. 43

p. 190 "Don't become . . . ", Ibid., p. 44.

p. 194 "On earth it happened . . .", Roland Bainton, *Here I Stand*, p. 353.

p. 197 "The Church everywhere presents a very sad picture . . ." John Nicholas Lenker, DD, *Luther's Two Catechisms*, pp. 6-7.

p. 197 "Faith is a . . . ", Roland Bainton, *Here I Stand*, p. 331.

p. 197 "It is well known that . . . ", Ibid., p. 325.

p. 198 "I am all right . . . ", Ibid., p. 327-28.

p. 198 "Translating is not something . . . ", Edith Simon, *Luther Alive*, p. 289.

p. 199 "I spent . . . ", Ibid., p. 342.

p. 199 "Even the noteless . . . ", Will Durant, *The Reformation*, p. 447.

p. 200 ""I have no use . . . ", Roland Bainton, *Here I Stand*, p. 341.

p. 203 "If I were a Jew . . . ", Ibid.

p. 205   "He became almost . . .", Will Durant, *The Reformation*, pp. 452-53.

p. 206   "Today at eight . . .", William Dallman, DD, *Kate Luther*, p. 100.

p. 206   "I wish you peace . . .", Ibid., p. 100.

p. 207   "To my dear housewife . . .", Ibid., p. 101.

p. 207   "To the holy, worrisome . . .", Julius Köstlin, *Martin Luther*, 547.

p. 207   "Dear Kate . . .", Edith Simon, *Luther Alive*, p. 351.

p. 208   "borne patiently . . .", Will Durant, *The Reformation*, p. 423 (Werke, [Erlangen] XVI in Allen, *Political Thought*).

p. 208   "Reverend father . . . Julius Köstlin, *Martin Luther*, p. 578.

p. 209   "The Monday after . . .", Gretzschel, Babovic, Ellert, & Verlag, *In Martin Luther's Footsteps*, p. 85.

p. 210   "God had given . . .", Joseph Stump, *Life of Philip Melanchthon*, p. 187.

p. 211   "Grace and peace . . .", William Dallman, *Kate Luther*, p. 105.

pp. 212-214   "I, Martin Luther . . .", Julius Köstlin, *Martin Luther*, p. 550. www.ndicms.org/finacialplanning/MartinLuther'swill.pdf (The original document was placed in the archives of the Evangelical Church of the Augsburg Confession in Budapest, Hungary.)

p. 215   "I have not come . . .", Henry Jacobs, *Martin Luther*, p. 409.

pp. 215-16   "I will abide . . .", Gustav Just, *Life of Luther*, p. 96.

pp. 218-19   "Katherine Bora is . . .", William Dallmann, DD, *Kate Luther*, p. 113.

p. 219   "During all her . . .", Ibid. p. 114.

BIBLIOGRAPHIC SOURCES

Apotheker, Jan and Livia Simon Sarkadi, eds., *European Women in Chemistry.* Wiley-VCH, 2011.

**Bainton, Roland H., *Here I Stand: A Life of Martin Luther,* Copyright by Pierce and Smith. New York and Nashville: Abingdon Press, 1952.

_____. *The Reformation of the Sixteenth Century.* Boston: The Beacon Press, 1952.

_____. *Women of the Reformation in Germany and Italy.* Philadelphia: Fortress Press, 1971.

_____. *Martin Luther's Christmas Book.* Minneapolis: Augsburg Books, 1997.

Bethge, Eberhard, *Dietrich Bonhoeffer—Letters and Papers from Prison.* New York: Macmillan Publishing, 1971.

Coole, Nathaniel, *Life of Martin Luther—A Sketch of the Rise & Progress of the Reformation in Germany.* London: Milford House, 1855.

Coulton, G. G., *Life in the Middle Ages I.* Cambridge, 1930.

Czamonske, Rev. William D. D., *400 Years.* St. Louis: Concordia Publishing House, 1916.

Dallmann, Dr. William, *Kate Luther.* Milwaukee: Northwestern Publishing House, 1941.

D'Aubigne, J. H. Merle, *History of the Great Reformation.* Milwaukee: Donohue & Co., 1901.

Dentler, Clara Louise, *Katherine Luther of the Wittenberg Parsonage.* Philadelphia: The United Lutheran Publishing House, 1924.

Durant, Will, *The Age of Faith.* New York: Simon and Schuster, 1950.

**_____. *The Reformation.* New York: Simon and Schuster, 1957.

Ernst, Richard, *History of German Civilization.* New York: The Macmillan Company, 1911.

Forster, John, *The Life of Charles Dickens: The Illustrated Edition.* New York: Sterling Publishing Co., Inc., 2011.

SOURCES

Fosdick, Harry Emerson, *Great Voices of the Reformation*. New York: Random House, 1932.

Fox, Robert, *Eyewitness to History: Discovering New Worlds*. London: The Folio Society Ltd., 2008.

Gay, Peter, *Age of Enlightenment*, Time-Life Books, Time Inc., 1966.

Gies, Frances and Joseph, *Life in a Medieval Village*. New York: Harper & Row Publishers, 1990.

Green, John Richard, *History of the English People*. Chicago and New York: Belford, Clarke & Co., 1886.

Gretzschel, Babovic, Ellert, & Verlag, *In Martin Luther's Footsteps*. Hamburg, Germany: Ellert and Richteer, 1996.

Grunwald, Henry, *Time*, Vol. 105, No. 20, New York: Time Inc., 1975.

Huckel, Dr. Oliver, *Richard Wagner, The Man and His Work*. New York: Thomas V. Crowell Company, Publishers, 1914.

Humphreys, H. Noel, *Intellectual Observer*, February 1862.

Hibbert, Christopher, *Rome: The Biography of a City, Chapter IX–"Patrons and Parasites"*. London: Viking Press, 1985.

Jacobs, Henry Eyster, *Martin Luther the Hero of the Reformation*. New York and London: G. P. Putnam's Sons and The Knickerbocker Press, 1898.

Janssen, Johannes, *History of the German People at the Close of the Middle Ages*. London: K. Paul, Trench, Tribner & Co. Ltd., 1896.

Just, Gustav, *Life of Luther*. St. Louis: Concordia Publishing House, 1905.

Karick, Jeff, *Forgotten English*, South Portland, ME: Sellers Publishing, Inc., 2012.

Koolman, WJ, *By Faith Alone*. Cambridge, UK: Lutterworth Press, 1954.

Kosiman, William J., *The Mature Luther*. Decorah, IA: Luther College Press, 1959.

**Kostlin, Julius, *Life of Luther*, Longmans. London: Green & Co., 1898.

Kunhardt, Jr., Philip B., Kunhardt III, Philip B., Kunhardt, Peter W. *Lincoln*. New York: Random House, 1992.

Lenker, John Nicholas, *Luther's Small Catechism*. Minneapolis: The Luther Press, 1908.

SOURCES

Lentz, Harold H., *Reformation Crossroads*. Minneapolis: Augsburg Publinging House, 1958.

Luther Bible as newly reviewed according to an approved text of a committee of the Evangelical Church in Germany.

Macauley, Lord Thomas Babington, *The History of England*, Vols. I & II. New York: Mason, Baker & Pratt, 1873.

Marius, Richard, *Martin Luther*. Cambridge, MA and London: The Belknap Press of Harvard University, 1999.

Morris, John G., *Catharine de Borea*. Philadelphia: Lindsay & Blakiston, 1856. 1999.

Moxey, Keith, *Peasants, Warriors, and Wives, Popular Imagery in the Reformation*, Chicago and London: Chicago Press, 1989.

Murphy, Cullen, "Torturer's Apprentice" in *The Atlantic*, January, February, 2012.

Nettl, Paul, *Luther in Music*. Philadelphia: The Muhlenberg Press, 1948.

Nohl, Frederick, *Martin Luther Hero of Faith*. St. Louis: Concordia Publishing House, 1962.

Plass, Ewald, *This is Luther*. St. Louis: Concordia Publishing, 1947.

Rasmussen, Lucy Gray, *Commencement Address*, May 24, 1923, Canton, SD.

Rosslin, Eucharius, *The Rosa Garden*. Germany, 1513.

Ogg, Frederic, *A Source Book of Medieval History: Documents Illustrative of European Life and Institutions from the German Invasions to the Renaissance*. New York: Cooper Square Publisher, 1972.

Paine, Thomas, *The Rights of Man*. Norwalk, CT: The Easton Press, 1972.

Pastor, Ludwig, *History of the Popes I*. London: Kegan Paul, Trench, Trübner & Co. LTD, London, 1906.

Schalk, Carl F., *Luther on Music: Paradigms of Praise*. St. Louis: Concordia Publishing House, 1988.

Schreiber, Clara Seuel, *Katherine, Wife of Luther*. Philadelphia: Muhlenberg Press, 1954.

Schuster, M. Lincoln, *The World's Great Letters*. New York: Simon and Schuster, 1940.

Schwiebert, E. G., *Luther and His Times*. St. Louis: Concordia Publishing, 1950.

SOURCES

Seebohm, Frederic, *The Era of the Protestant Revolution.* New York: Charles Scribner's Sons, 1900.

Service Book and Hymnal, Minneapolis: Augsburg Publishing House, 1958.

Severy, Merle, "*The World of Martin Luther*," *National Geographic Magazine*, October 1983. Washington DC: National Geographic Society.

Simon, Edith, *The Reformation, Great Ages of Man, A History of the World's Cultures.* New York: Time, Inc., 1966.

**_____. *Luther Alive: Martin Luther and the Making of the Reformation.* New York: Doubleday & Company, Inc., 1968.

Smith, Jeanette C., *Katherine von Bora Through Five Centuries, A Historiography.* Carlsbad, NM: New Mexico State University, 1999.

Stump, Joseph, *Life of Philip Melanchthon.* Reading, PA: Pilger Publishing House, 1897.

Wacknerngel, William, *The Life of Martin Luther.* Lebanon PA: The Pilger Book Store, 1883.

Wecker, Johann Jacob, *Secrets of Art and Nature I-XVIII*, augmented & translated by Dr. R. Read, London; printed and plagiarized by Simon Miller, 1661.

Webster's Ninth New Collegiate Dictionary. Springfield, MA: Merriman-Webster Inc., 1988.

Worsley, Henry, *The Life of Martin Luther, vol. 2.* London: Bell and Daldy, 1856.

** *Recommended for further in-depth study*